RESTORED to LEAD

A Self-Leadership Manual to Break Free from
Burnout and Renew Your Purpose

Phillip G Andrade

AUXANO

COPYRIGHTS

RESTORED TO LEAD

A Self-Leadership Manual to Break Free from Burnout
and Renew Your Purpose

For Patty

To the greatest blessing God ever gave to me.

My best friend, helpmate and partner in shenanigans.

TABLE OF CONTENTS

INTRODUCTORY NOTE

The following is not a comprehensive manual on self-care for the church leader. There are plenty of great books and studies out there that can give you a foundation for this important topic. In these pages I am discussing, what I believe to be, the most common areas where pastors fall short in their self-care. These insights come from my personal life and the struggles of other leaders that I know. I hope this book and its simple tools will give you some basic starting points to begin the journey of restoration where you can lead those entrusted to you in the power of His Spirit. This manual does not promise a solution to all the ills of every pastor out there but what it does promise is a starting point for a new journey with Jesus.

The photos throughout the book are from my personal travels and times of renewal. I hope they inspire you to live well and fully for Jesus.

I have been crucified with Christ
and I no longer live,
but Christ lives in me.
The life I now live in the body,
I live by faith in the Son of God,
who loved me
and gave himself for me.
Galatians 2:20

MY STORY

01

MY STORY

Many Pastors I talk to believe, at least on the inside, that being a faithful pastor means giving everything you have—time, energy, even health—until there was nothing left. I too thought exhaustion was a sign of commitment. Sleepless nights were worth it. After all I was doing it for Jesus. I told myself that running on empty meant I was doing God's work.

I had heard a quote attributed to the missionary Amy Carmichael. As a young Christian and it inspired me. "I'd rather burn out (for Jesus) than rust out," she said. That sounded so spiritual to me. Then, one morning, I woke up and realized I couldn't do it anymore. I was burned out for Jesus. The joy of ministry was gone. Preparing a sermon was a struggle. Prayer had become work, not a cry of my heart to God. I had poured out so much that I was completely empty inside.

And then it happened: My body broke down. I ended up in the hospital for over a week with diverticulitis. The doctors said it was stress related. I remember lying there, staring at the ceiling, knowing they were right. The way I was living—rushing, pushing, never resting—wasn't sustainable. I was serving hard but not living well and it wasn't spiritual at all. I was reminded that Jesus said following him would mean a burden (Matthew 11:29-30) but the burden was supposed to be light and with that burden we would have rest. This was not light at all. I wasn't finding rest. It felt like death.

That moment was the beginning of a new understanding about what it means to take care of oneself holistically as an act of worship and sustainability in ministry. God didn't fix me overnight, but He began something new in me—a slow, grace-filled journey toward health. I had to learn that caring for my soul and body wasn't selfish. It was part of my calling.

Many pastors carry this same idea of faithfulness - Serve Jesus until you burn out. We preach rest in Jesus but rarely rest ourselves. We counsel others to stop being such a workaholic while hiding our own exhaustion. We talk about joy but live with mild depression. This book is born from that struggle—the desire to serve God without losing myself in the process. It's about learning to live biblically again. To care for the mind, body, and spirit that make up who we are as shepherds of God's people.

My prayer is that as you read, you'll find courage to slow down, grace to heal, and space to rediscover joy in the call God has given to you. Living for Jesus was never meant to destroy us—it was meant to shape us into His likeness.

So that's my story in a nutshell, maybe it's your story too.

Beloved, I pray that in all respects you may prosper and be in good health, just as your soul prospers. 3 John 1:2

Phil

RESTORED TO LEAD

Phillip G Andrade

Beloved,
I pray that in all respects you may prosper and be in good health, just as your soul prospers.
3 John 1:2

THE PHYSICAL NEEDS
OF THE PASTOR

02

THE PHYSICAL NEEDS OF THE PASTOR

"...and you shall love the Lord your God with all your heart, and with all your soul, and with all your mind, and with all your strength."Mark 12:30

We are human. We are dust. The bodies that we live in now are earthly though they will one day give way to spiritual bodies. But that day is not now so we have to take care of the body God has blessed us with. To love God with our strength is a call to steward our bodies, minds, and spirits faithfully. Ministry requires more than passion—it requires wholeness. Sustainable leadership depends on disciplined care for the body and soul.

Taking care of our bodies is not just a suggestion but a command that God gives us. Paul in writing to the church in Corinth says clearly:

Or do you not know that your body is a sanctuary of the Holy Spirit who is in you, whom you have from God, and that you are not your own? For you were bought with a price: therefore glorify God in your body. 1 Cor 6:19-20

Some may point out that the verse doesn't say literally to "take care" of your body but one cannot glorify God with a body that is being or has been abused and neglected. Paul uses the idea that taking care of our bodies is equated with that which is of the utmost importance.

THE PHYSICAL NEEDS OF THE PASTOR

So husbands ought also to love their own wives as their own bodies. He who loves his own wife loves himself; for no one ever hated his own flesh, but nourishes and cherishes it, just as Christ also does the church, Eph 5:28-29

Taking care of our physical bodies is something that is so important that Paul uses it as an example to show the way Jesus cares for his Bride. The self care of our bodies should not be secondary to one who is called to lead others. In fact, much of the Bible talks about this area in specific ways. Modern Christians tend to ignore these verses. When was the last time you heard a sermon on gluttony or sexual sins against the body? (Pro 23:20-21, Phil 3:19, 1 Cor 6:15-18)

We have been taught that our souls/spirits and bodies are separate things so we need to focus on the spirit over all else. And while the trichotomist vs dichotomist nature of man is an interesting topic to discuss theologically, practically the Scriptures teach emphatically that we are unified beings. When our spirits depart at death to be with Jesus, we wait for the resurrection of our bodies. We were not meant to live a compartmentalized life.

God seeks to shape us into the image of Jesus holistically. One example of this is from 1 Thessalonians:

Now may the God of peace Himself sanctify you entirely, and may your spirit and soul and body be preserved complete, without blame at the coming of our Lord Jesus Christ. 1 Thess 5:23

Of course there is a danger for some of us. Some of us may so focus on the physical that we ignore the spiritual needs of or lives. This can become idolatry. Yet, my experience in talking with pastors is that they err on physical neglect that leads to spiritual decline. It rarely works the other way around. Paul's advice to a young pastor is important to bring into this discussion.

for bodily training is only of little profit, but godliness is profitable for all things, since it holds promise for the present life and also for the life to come. 1 Tim 4:8

The purpose here is to let you know that it is ok to take care of your body. It is not carnal but rather one of the most important things we can do to help us grow closer to Jesus. We are not compartmentalized beings. When we offer our bodies we offer our whole selves - soul, spirit and body. The one area of our lives that is neglected will bleed out onto the others. The result is a spiraling burnout that may, at the least, harm your ministry and at the worst, harm others that God has placed in your care.

Let's look at some practical strategies we can adopt to ensure that we are glorifying God with our bodies.

THE FORGOTTEN DISCIPLINE OF REST

It is in vain that you rise up early, That you sit out late, O you who eat the bread of painful labors;For in this manner, He gives sleep to His beloved. Psalm 127:2

Sleep is not a luxury; it is a necessity built into the very rhythm of creation. God Himself modeled rest after His work (Genesis 2:2–3). Yet many pastors live as though rest were optional, sacrificing sleep for ministry demands. Sometimes sleep is neglected because ministry demands early hours and late nights but more often than not, the lack of sleep is due to a restless mind and a burdened heart. I cannot count the number of times I could not sleep because my mind ran through all the things I did and did not do that day. I relived all the things that I said that were ineffective or worse hurt someone deeply. I wept inside over the times I did not stand for the truth or used the truth as a weapon to get people to conform to my wishes. And then there were the burdens. All the hurt and pain of people in my congregation - their struggles and patterns of life that I could not change but wanted to (More on this later: the tendency to take on responsibilities that are not mine). There was the burden or more accurately, the guilt of neglecting my wife and children "for the sake of the ministry." So when my head hit the pillow many nights my mind went into high gear and sleep did not come or was interrupted.

Recently, I was blessed by my church to have a three-month sabbatical. It was the first one I have had in over 40 years of ministry. I'll talk more about the need for sabbatical in a later chapter but for now I wanted to give you an insight into how my sleep habits changed during my three months off.

The first full day of my sabbatical I was alone at a summer home. I went to bed that night for the first time free from worrying what to do tomorrow or what issues I needed to deal with. That night I went to bed with a relatively quiet mind. I woke up 15hours later. I don't mean I sleep off and on for 15 hours. I slept for 15 hours straight. My body said you need this when my mind allowed it. As I wrote this section, I am at my desk exactly one day in back from my sabbatical. One of the things that I am determined to change is my sleeping habits. As I have eluded to, this has much to do with the mental health and state of your thought life. We will delve into that shortly. For now I want to simply state that sleep and physical rest are not laziness. They are a declaration of faith. When we can put our work aside and not take our burdens to bed we are saying that I trust that God can take care of HIS church while I am asleep. That responsibility is not mine. It is his. I must learn to trust God enough to sleep.

When rest and sleep are neglected, the effects can cascade:

PHYSICALLY

Lack of sleep significantly undermines how the brain works—attention, memory, decision making, emotional regulation all suffer.

A recent study found that sleep disruptions affect attention, memory consolidation (both NREM & REM sleep), impulse control and increase emotional reactivity.[1] According to National Heart, Lung, and Blood Institute, lack of sleep or rest raises risk of chronic conditions such as hypertension, heart disease and stroke.[2] A report by Harvard Health noted that people sleeping less than 6 hours a night have nearly 3 times the risk of heart disease. There is even some mounting evidence that it may be linked to increased risk of dementia.[3] Other studies show associations with higher blood pressure, obesity, immune-function decline, and cancer risks.[4]

Long term lack of sleep and rest not only impact short term ministry but can sideline a pastor long term or permanently. We have one body to serve with so we must be serious about its care. An early death or major illness has removed a pastor from ministry all too often.

[1] Hyndych, A., El-Abassi, R., and Mader, E. C., Jr. "The Role of Sleep and the Effects of Sleep Loss on Cognitive, Affective, and Behavioral Processes." *Cureus* 17, no. 5 (May 16, 2025): e84232. https://doi.org/10.7759/cureus.84232. PMID: 40525051; PMCID: PMC12168795.

[2] National Heart, Lung, and Blood Institute. "Sleep Deprivation and Deficiency." National Institutes of Health. Accessed December 28, 2025. https://www.nhlbi.nih.gov/health/sleep-deprivation/health-effects

[3] Harvard Health Publishing. "How Sleep Deprivation Can Harm Your Health." Harvard Health Blog. Accessed December 28, 2025. https://www.health.harvard.edu/staying-healthy/how-sleep-deprivation-can-harm-your-health.

[4] Johns Hopkins Medicine. "The Effects of Sleep Deprivation." Johns Hopkins Medicine Health Library. Accessed December 28, 2025. https://www.hopkinsmedicine.org/health/wellness-and-prevention/the-effects-of-sleep-deprivation.

MENTALLY:

Insufficient sleep is closely linked to mood disturbances and longer-term mental-health issues: In a large US population-based study, adults averaging less than 6 hours a night of sleep had about 2.5 times higher odds of frequent mental distress compared to those with over 6 hours of sleep.[5]

Other studies show acute sleep deprivation increases anxiety, depressive symptoms and general distress.[6] This trend is not just found in one study but many. Another found that short sleep duration is a risk factor for depression, anxiety, and other mental-wellbeing issues.[7]

This data is important for pastors and leaders to understand. Much of ministry involves discernment and good judgment. The lack of sleep will cloud and distort these very important skills. For a pastor to have a long-term sustainable ministry stable mood regulation, emotional resilience, and mental-health maintenance all depend on adequate sleep. Poor sleep may not only trigger bad moods and irritability short-term, but over the long-term increase vulnerability to serious mental-health disorders and an ineffective calling.

PASTORAL PHYSICAL HEALTH CRISIS

59% of pastors say consistently exercising is a challenge.

49% of pastors report struggling to eat healthy.

80% sometimes sacrifice their own wellbeing.

[5] Centers for Disease Control and Prevention. "The Effects of Sleep Deprivation on Health." Preventing Chronic Disease 18 (2021). Accessed December 28, 2025. https://www.cdc.gov/pcd/issues/2021/20_0573.htm.

[6] Babson, K. A., Trainor, C. D., Feldner, M. T., and Blumenthal, H. "A Test of the Effects of Acute Sleep Deprivation on General and Specific Self-Reported Anxiety and Depressive Symptoms: An Experimental Extension." Journal of Behavioral Therapy and Experimental Psychiatry 41, no. 3 (September 2010): 297-303. https://doi.org/10.1016/j.jbtep.2010.02.008. Epub February 23, 2010. PMID: 20231014; PMCID: PMC2862829.

[7] Shah, A. S., Pant, M. R., Bommasamudram, T., Nayak, K. R., Roberts, S. S. H., Gallagher, C., Vaishali, K., Edwards, B. J., Tod, D., Davis, F., and Pullinger, S. A. "Effects of Sleep Deprivation on Physical and Mental Health Outcomes: An Umbrella Review." American Journal of Lifestyle Medicine (May 27, 2025): 15598276251346752. https://doi.org/10.1177/15598276251346752. Epub ahead of print. PMID: 40443808; PMCID: PMC12116485.

SPIRITUALLY

In a study of 190 hemodialysis patients, poorer sleep quality (measured by the Pittsburgh Sleep Quality Index) was significantly positively correlated with lower spiritual well-being.[8]

I could list other studies as well, but it is not rocket science to see the impact that lack of sleep on our spiritual lives. When our bodies and mental health are shot there is only one thing left to be damaged. Our walk with Jesus. Remember, even Jesus slept during the storm.

That day when evening came, he said to his disciples, "Let us go over to the other side." Leaving the crowd behind, they took him along, just as he was, in the boat. There were also other boats with him. A furious squall came up, and the waves broke over the boat, so that it was nearly swamped. Jesus was in the stern, sleeping on a cushion. The disciples woke him and said to him,

"Teacher, do You not care that we are perishing?" And He woke up and rebuked the wind and said to the sea, "Silence! Be still." And the wind died down and it became perfectly calm. And He said to them, "Why are you so cowardly? Do you still have no faith?" Mark 4:38b-40

In this passage we rightly focus on Jesus divine power, yet there is more going on here. The disciples are working hard, (like we do in ministry) trying to get a handle on the storm around them wondering if God cares enough to save them. The answer comes in with the statement Jesus was in the stern, sleeping on a cushion. Why mention this side note to the story of a miracle of divine power? Here's the key. It's not a side note. It's the point. The disciples are trying to manage the storm and wearing themselves out. Jesus demonstrates divine trust by sleeping. God is in control of the storm so he can rest safely and then show power in ministry. A sleeping Jesus models trust in the one who is in control. I can let things go and rest well knowing God is sovereign. Faith can express itself through physical rest.

Sleep is not the only area of the physical pastors need to focus on. We not only need rest. We need energy.

[8] Eslami, A. A., Rabiei, L., Khayri, F., Rashidi Nooshabadi, M. R., and Masoudi, R. "Sleep Quality and Spiritual Well-Being in Hemodialysis Patients." Iranian Red Crescent Medical Journal 16, no. 7 (July 2014): e17155. https://doi.org/10.5812/ircmj.17155. Epub July 5, 2014. PMID: 25237580; PMCID: PMC4166099.

NOURISHING THE TEMPLE

Or do you not know that your body is a sanctuary of the Holy Spirit who is in you, whom you have from God, and that you are not your own? For you were bought with a price: therefore glorify God in your body. 1 Cor 6:19–20

As we have discussed, Paul's theology of the body reveals that our physical health is deeply spiritual. As temples of the Holy Spirit, our bodies are to be used for the glory of God. He wants his temple to shine so that others might be drawn to him. A run-down shack just won't do. Simply stated, neglecting our body dishonors the God who dwells within.

Eating healthy shows a daily stewardship of this temple God has honored us with. Healthy eating is not gluttony or overindulgence. It can be worship. We worship God by treating things that are holy with reverence.

Therefore I exhort you, brothers, by the mercies of God, to present your bodies as a sacrifice—living, holy, and pleasing to God, which is your spiritual service of worship..Rom 12:1

Offering our whole self (including our bodies) is a holy act and equals true worship. Sacred things must be kept sacred. One of the principles in the book of Leviticus was to make sure that the things that were considered holy not be mixed or defiled by the profane. I think the principle carries over. We dishonor God when we take our bodies and profane them by eating in an unhealthy way.

God calls us to treat that which he has made holy (our bodily temple) with reverence and care. I know we have busy lives. I don't know how often I have stuffed my face with fast food because that's "all I had time for." I know pastors are often way underpaid and buying healthy food can seem like the food budget has been spent way before its time. We can be rushed and eating healthy can be expensive, but we have to find a way and develop strategies rather than use excuses to not honor God with our bodies. So, we need to tweak the question bit. We should not ask "What do I have time or money to eat?" but rather "What honors the One who inhabits my body for I am not my own. I have been brought with a price?"

We have an interesting narrative in Daniel 1 that may help us with this conundrum. Daniel and his friends were brought into the court of King Nebuchadnezzar. They were to be trained for service in the court and as such lived there. Of course, that meant that they had to eat what was given to them. Or did they?

But Daniel set in his heart that he would not defile himself with the king's choice food or with the wine which he drank; so he sought permission from the commander of the officials that he might not defile himself. Dan 1:8

Now the context is a little different than most modern situations. The Scripture uses the word "defile" (לגאל) which has a ritual connotation. So, the food given them was either a forbidden type in the Torah or was sacrificed to idols. Notice that Daniel didn't make excuses about his time or position. He simply chose to sacrifice. To do what God wanted and trust God for the results. And God gave the results because of their faithfulness to his Word and call.

At the end of ten days it was seen that their appearance was better and that they were fatter than all the youths who had been eating the king's choice food. Dan 1:15

To these four young men God gave knowledge and understanding of all kinds of literature and learning. And Daniel could understand visions and dreams of all kinds (Dan 1:17).

Daniels sacrifice and conviction, to do what was right, directly led to strength (Physical) and metal clarity. I firmly believe if we resolve to honor God by what we put in our bodies, no matter what we may have to sacrifice, we will find strength and clarity for ministry.

As with the discipline of rest, we can swing the pendulum too far. The Scripture is replete with warnings against gluttony and overindulgence (Proverbs 23:20–21). Even eating healthy can become an idol if our focus becomes one of self-gratification rather than glorifying God.

Your diet will influence your mood, energy, and spiritual attentiveness. The foods you choose either support your ministry or slowly erode it. We should all want to nourish our bodies so that they will serve the Lord not only well, but with distinction.

THE GIFT OF MOVEMENT

for bodily training is only of little profit, but godliness is profitable for all things, since it holds promise for the present life and also for the life to come.. 1 Timothy 4:8

Paul acknowledges the "value" of physical training as a legitimate part of discipleship. Studies have shown that exercise strengthens not only the body but also the mind and spirit.[9]

I admit, exercise is hard for me. I don't enjoy it unless it includes a walk in the woods during deer season. When I was younger it was much easier. Playing volleyball and softball kept me in shape and provided the aerobic exercise I needed. Now my knees can't take the impact of volleyball and if I slide into home plate I will almost certainly need a cast and traction. I also will admit that when I do exercise, I feel 200% better. So, I force myself to put in the 10-15 minutes a day to strengthen my back and other areas that don't work quite like they used to. That discipline and a walk down the street with my wife 2 or 3 times during the week keep me in the 200% better world.

I also know that that the rhythm that I need will sometimes give way to old patterns that if I am honest, are simply laziness. If you have been a Christian, any length of time, you may be as adept as I am in making sin look like the most spiritual thing ever. I don't have time to exercise, there is an emergency that I must get to, a prayer I have to pray, a Bible I need to read. It's not that those tasks are bad it's the attitude behind them. Charles Hummel wrote a little booklet entitled "The Tyranny of the Urgent."

PASTORAL FRIENDSHIPS

70% of pastors say they have no close friends.

61% of pastors have "a few close friends."

70% of pastors say that they believe friendships are vital in ministry.

[9] Chekroud, S. R., Gueorguieva, R., Zheutlin, A. B., Paulus, M., Krumholz, H. M., Krystal, J. H., and Chekroud, A. M. "Association Between Physical Exercise and Mental Health in 1.2 Million Individuals in the USA Between 2011 and 2015: A Cross-Sectional Study." The Lancet Psychiatry 5, no. 9 (September 2018): 739-746. https://doi.org/10.1016/S2215-0366(18)30227-X. Epub August 8, 2018. PMID: 30099000.
Konopack, J. F., and McAuley, E. "Efficacy-Mediated Effects of Spirituality and Physical Activity on Quality of Life: A Path Analysis." Health and Quality of Life Outcomes 10 (May 29, 2012): 57. https://doi.org/10.1186/1477-7525-10-57. PMID: 22642832; PMCID: PMC3406955.

THE PHYSICAL NEEDS OF THE PASTOR

That little booklet summarizes the attitude. We spend our lives and resources on the urgent things rather than the really important things. It's the spiritual equivalent of the squeaky wheel gets the oil. When we rush off to take care of the urgent (That may not be urgent at all in the scheme of things) we sacrifice that which is of greater importance. It is not godly to be rushing around at the whim of the urgent. The godly thing it to have a set of biblical priorities that will truly set us free. The health of our bodies should be one of those priorities. If we do not exercise, we will not last for the long haul. Our bodies will give out long before our passion for the gospel does. In addition, we will have no energy to respond to the truly urgent.

Like sleep and eating healthy, there are real benefits of regular exercise:

- It increases energy and mental clarity.

- It reduces harmful stress and supports emotional balance.

- It can result in longer life and therefore longer ministry.

In 1 Corinthians 9:24–27, Paul uses the metaphor of an athlete to describe spiritual discipline.

> *Do you not know that those who run in a race all run, but only one receives the prize? Run in such a way that you may win. Now everyone who competes in the games exercises self-control in all things. They then do it to receive a corruptible crown, but we an incorruptible. Therefore I run in such a way, as not without aim; I box in such a way, as not beating the air; but I discipline my body and make it my slave, so that, after I have preached to others, I myself will not be disqualified.*
> *1 Cor 9:24-27*

Like an athlete, a pastor must train for endurance, not for short bursts of energy. Exercise, when viewed as stewardship, becomes another form of worship—thanking God for strength and mobility.

THE NECESSITY OF DEEP FRIENDSHIPS

Iron sharpens iron, So one man sharpens another.Proverbs 27:17

Leadership can be lonely. Many pastors are surrounded by people yet live in relational isolation. This has been true of me for many of the years I have been in ministry. I tend to be introverted so making deep friendships has always been a challenge to me. Add to that character quality the circumstances and challenges that surround many pastors it becomes difficult find and maintain friendships. That is highly problematic. Though I'm not a person that has many deep friendships I have been blessed enough to have a few close long-time friends, a devoted wife and a few mentors that give me the relational outlets to process my life and ministry. Let's step back from my story and ask the question why this seems to be chronic in many pastors' lives? Barna research has conducted many studies over the years on this problem. One of the most recent found that 70% of pastors have no close friends.[10]

There are many reasons for this, unfortunately, downward trend.

FEAR OF VULNERABILITY

There is a constant demand to appear strong in every area of life that often prevents genuine friendships. We hide our hurts and concerns under the guise of professionalism. We cry out inside, "I have a job to do and I must put on my pastoral persona to be who I need to be for the situation. No way do I feel safe to be the real me." Leaders often feel that it is unsafe to be self. The result is a life that is not congruent. We can't let people in to know the true me and still put on the pastoral mask. C. Michael Thompson in the preface of his book "The Congruent Life," calls this tension spiritual pain.

"It was the pain of being separated from my authentic self. Of having to live someone else's life in order to "go along and get along." that well-trod, sequential career path.[11]"

This fear of being our true selves means that no one can really know us and therefore friendships that meet our inmost needs are never realized.

[10] Barna Group. "Rest and the Sabbath." Barna Research. Accessed December 28, 2025. https://www.barna.com/research/rest-sabbath/.

[11] Thompson, C. Michael. The Congruent Life: Following the Inward Path to Fulfilling Work and Inspired Leadership. San Francisco: Jossey-Bass, 2000.

FEAR OF BETRAYAL

Unfortunately, it happens all too often. We open up ourselves and try to be authentic, vulnerable so we can be who we really are, and someone comes along and takes advantage of it. They use that very vulnerability that should bring healing and congruence into our lives and use it to hurt and destroy us, our family and even our ministry. Most of the time they don't really mean to. They are trying to deal with their disfunctions just like we are, but it hurts deeply none the less.

Over the years I have felt the sting of betrayal many times. Many times, I could just brush it off. After all I have unknowingly hurt people too. The discipline of forgiveness is so important for a pastor to know well. But there was the one time where a betrayal hurt so deep that it affected me for years (and if I'm honest, still affects me to this day). The betrayal looked like the right thing to do. It was couched in spiritual language and the accusations of not loving enough without giving any details. The betrayal was so deep it not only cut short that ministry but also deeply tarnished my children's view of the church. That hurt so bad because I loved the church. The betrayal wasn't by the whole church, it was only a few but it impacted everything and everyone I loved. I thought of leaving the ministry completely but God in his mercy led me to another church where I and my family could heal. For years it took a lot to be my real self even in this new place of ministry. It happened before; it could happen again is the constant refrain that will go through my brain.

Though there have not been many focused studies on pastoral betrayal. Some reports find that roughly about 1 in 4 pastors say they have been fired or forced to resign at some point in their careers.[12]

Factions that force pastors are often very small. In one study, 43% of forced-out pastors said a "small faction" forced them out, and 71% of those pastors said that faction numbered 10 or fewer congregants. As in my experience it is often a small proportion of church members that can cause a pastor's removal.[13]

Probably the most shocking statistic is that the average pastoral tenure in a local church today is just 3.8 years.[14]

There is a sense among many pastors that it we even give an inch we will find a knife in the back, so we seclude ourselves and suffer the consequences of a lack of friendships. This is not what God wants for us.

[12] Columbia Theological Seminary. "Columbia Seminary Addresses an Epidemic of Clergy in Crisis." Columbia Theological Seminary. Accessed December 28, 2025. https://www.ctsnet.edu/columbia-seminary-addresses-an-epidemic-of-clergy-in-crisis/.
[13] ibid
[14] Ibid.

Oil and incense make the heart glad, So counsel from the soul is sweet to his friend. Proverbs 27:9

ABANDONMENT DYSFUNCTION

My father's father died when he was very young. His stepdad died a few years after he returned home from World War II, when he was only 21. Luckily, my father lived until his late 80s, but I still felt abandoned. My dad was a construction crane operator and was often away for weeks at a job. Some of my most precious memories were of me and my mom visiting him at what seemed to be exotic places of work. I remember vividly one day my dad brought a gift home from work with him for me. It was back in the day when gas stations used to give out toys for a certain number of fill ups. This toy happened to be a tractor trailer filled with plastic boxes and other sorts of gear that would be shipped in that truck. One of those little plastic pieces was in the shape of a piece of luggage. When I received that toy, I was overjoyed, but I immediately removed all the luggage and threw them in the trash. They reminded me of every time my dad would pack his suitcase and leave for weeks on end.

I thought nothing of these family stories until I started experiencing a deep sense of abandonment when somebody in my congregation would leave. I'm not talking about people leaving because they found something wrong with the church but rather people just leaving because they moved, got a job someplace else or other similar situations. None of those circumstances could I pin on myself as the cause but nonetheless, I felt abandoned by them. With some deep self-analysis I've come to the conclusion that in my inner being I have this great fear of being abandoned by those that I love. It seems that it's been passed on generation to generation in different ways. My father expressed these thoughts as well, though he wouldn't necessarily have used the word abandonment to describe them. This dynamic of dysfunctions in our lives, especially feelings of abandonment or poor self-image can cause us to retreat into ourselves and not seek out friendships for the sole reason that we don't want to lose those friendships. We protect ourselves from those feelings of loss. This type, of dysfunction, not only impacts potential friendships but also the level of intimacy in our closest relationships.

It important to realize that Jesus cultivated close relationships. Among the twelve, He counted Peter, James, and John as his inner circle and his closest friends. In His most sorrowful moments, He sought their companionship and support (Matthew 26:37–38). Even more precious to me are Jesus' words in John 15:14:

You are My friends if you do what I command you.

THE PHYSICAL NEEDS OF THE PASTOR

When Jesus talks about great intimacy in human relationships he most often goes to friendships rather and marriage and family.

No longer do I call you slaves, for the slave does not know what his master is doing; but I have called you friends, for all things that I have heard from My Father I have made known to you. John 15:15

Jesus wants me as his friend. In that passage Jesus equates friendship with openness. "You are my friends so I letting you know everything about what is most important to me." Now obviously, friendship with Jesus is much different than human to human friendship. We are not equals with Jesus but the principal holds. Friendship means we can be completely open about everything and there is freedom in that. In that garden before he was crucified, Jesus would rather have gone through the storm with his friends than without them.

Healthy, deep friendships for pastors are more than just a nice addition to life. They are essential because they can become spiritual lifelines when there is nothing else to hold on to. Don't ever forget that the primary way Jesus ministers to us is through his Body, the church. I hope that if you are married you find your wife is your best friend. I believe that is the way God designed marriage. Our greatest support should come from our helpmate. But know this: you need more than your wife.

If you think like me you may say, "Well I'm a loner, I don't need many friends." Don't deceive yourself. Being a loner is much different than being lonely. If we don't find deep friendships, the gap that God designed those relationships to fill may get filled with something else like, depression, hurt and bitterness. You deserve better and so do the people in your church that God has entrusted to you.

Two are better than one because they have good wages for their labor. For if either of them falls, the one will lift up his companion. But woe to the one who falls when there is not a second one to lift him up. Eccl 4:9–10

True friendship supplies us with much that we need to survive the difficulties of ministry such as:

• **Mutual Encouragement:** We need friends who speak truth and grace into our lives and give us an avenue to grow in the fruit of encouragement.

• **Accountability:** Surrounding yourself with "yes men" is never good for ministry. We need friends who will lovingly challenge us and help us refine our plans and own up to our shortcomings.

- **Safety:** Friends allow us to be our true self. They give us spaces where authenticity replaces performance building islands of refreshing into our ministry.

- **Joy:** Fun. Having a friend to share the journey and who enjoys the same stupid things you enjoy is a great blessing. It refreshes our soul just to spend time eating together, fishing, whatever floats your proverbial boat.

If you are a leader that is lonely you are vulnerable. Deep biblical friendships are not optional. They can protect us from a great fall.

THE RHYTHM OF SABBATH

Remember the sabbath day, to keep it holy. Exodus 20:8

Come away by yourselves to a desolate place and rest a while. Mark 6:31

When we hear the word, Sabbath most protestants shudder. Sabbath of evokes images of the law in a works-based faith. But that reaction is unwarranted. The principle of the Sabbath begins a long time before the law was given to Moses. Its foundation is in the very creation itself.

By the seventh day God had finished the work he had been doing; so on the seventh day he rested from all his work. Then God blessed the seventh day and made it holy, because on it he rested (shabath שָׁבַת) from all the work of creating that he had done. Gen 2:2-3

The word shabath (שָׁבַת) has a range of meanings from "to cease," "to rest," and of course "to observe" the Sabbath Day. Though as Christians we don't observe the Sabbath Day as prescribed in the Law, we need to understand that there is a rhythm of rest founded at the creation. God established a rhythm of work and rest in creation itself long before the law came into existence. Yes, Jesus is the ultimate fulfillment of the Sabbath (Mark 2:28) yet if we ignore that which is programmed into creation then as creatures we will suffer. To adopt the rhythm of sabbath into our lives means we stop striving, we rest in God's provision not in our productivity, and remind ourselves that the church belongs to Christ, not to us. Practicing sabbath is an act of worship in that it declares faith in God as the ultimate provider: We acknowledge a reliance on God to provide for our needs, freeing us from the need to work constantly to earn security. When we cease from work, we rediscover who we are apart from what we produce. Sabbath will humble us and reminds us that ministry is a partnership with God, not a performance for Him.

The practice of sabbath is not a day—it is a rhythm of renewal. These rhythms can take many forms:

THE PHYSICAL NEEDS OF THE PASTOR

- **Daily Sabbath:** Brief pauses for prayer and reflection during your normal work schedule.

- **Weekly Sabbath:** A full day to rest, worship, and reconnect. Most pastors take at least a day off yet also confess that they still take calls and will go to work at the office if needed on those days. Make it a priority that this doesn't happen otherwise you will just have a pseudo-sabbath which is no sabbath at all.

- **Seasonal/Yearly Sabbaths:** Extended times for retreat and refreshment. These could be a weekend away quarterly or even a week of rest. It should not be your typical vacation. Vacations are not sabbaticals, nor would I characterize most of them with the word restful. Vacation and enjoying family should be part of your life but they are not a sabbatical rhythm. This practice is about stopping the normal busyness of life to focus on the Lord. They are not about replacing one kind of busyness with another kind. My present church provides me with several vacation weeks and one week for study, renewal and sabbath. I frequently use that week to go alone on a retreat.

- **Seven-year Sabbath:** After over 40 years of ministry, I was blessed with a three-month sabbatical. I don't want to get into a lot of details because I am still processing all that I learned and experienced as I write this, but I will say this. The sabbatical saved my ministry at the church. I felt the progress of burnout moving in again and my church responded with an extended time away. It is essential for pastors to get away for the pressures of decades long 24/7 ministry. Each church should have a clear sabbatical policy. I would suggest a 3-4 month extended time away every seventh year. If the sabbatical is any shorter in length, the leader will not have enough time to fully disengage from his normal pattern of life to rest, renew and process.

If a church leader does not disengage from the unhealthy practice of overwork (the needs will always be there no matter how much we strive), constant stress and the pressure to be professional in every way, burnout is inevitable. The practice of a rhythm of sabbatical can be the most important discipline a leader can develop to sustain a long-term and fruitful ministry.

In this next section we are going to do some refection on the principles above as well as take some assessments to help discern where we might be on the road to potential burnout. It is of utmost importance to engage with the discussion above on a personal level. If we want to be healthy then it will take some courageousness to honestly look in areas of our lives that we may not be so excited to examine.

PRINCIPLES

1 **REST:** Sleep is a discipline of trust in God.

2 **HEALTHY EATING:** Caring for our bodies is an act of worship in honoring God's temple.

3 **EXERCISE:** Exercise increases endurance and mental clarity.

4 **FRIENDSHIPS**: Deep friendships provide accountability and safety.

5 **SABBATH RHYTHM:** Sabbath provides renewal and increases our trust in God's sovereign control.

STEP 1:

ASSESS YOUR BURNOUT DANGER LEVEL

This inventory is designed to access your risk of burnout in the areas that have to do with your physical health. It will examine the five key areas we talked about : Sleep & Rest, Healthy Eating, Exercise & Health, Deep Friendships, and Sabbath Rhythms.

Each question should be scored on a scale of 1 to 10, where:

1 = Strongly Disagree / Rarely True

10 = Strongly Agree / Consistently True

This inventory is not scientific but simply a tool to give you starting point to ask the hard questions

Section 1: Sleep and Rest

I regularly get 7–8 hours of quality sleep each night.

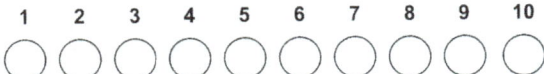

I wake up feeling refreshed and ready for the day.

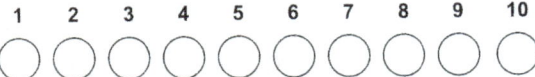

I maintain a consistent sleep schedule, even on weekends.

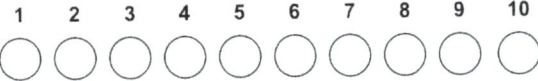

I allow myself to rest when I am tired rather than pushing through exhaustion

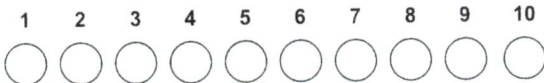

I take intentional breaks during the day to recharge mentally and physically..

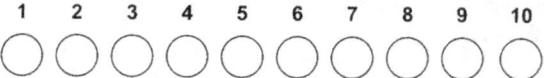

Subtotal (Add 1-10 for each): ____ / 50

Section 2: Healthy Eating

I eat balanced meals that include fruits, vegetables, and whole foods.

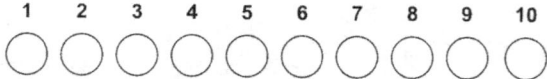

I avoid relying on fast food or processed snacks due to time or stress.

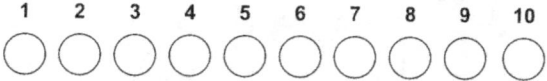

I stay adequately hydrated throughout the day.

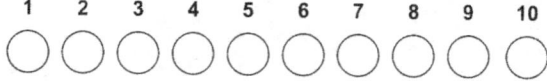

I make time for regular meals instead of skipping them to meet ministry demands.

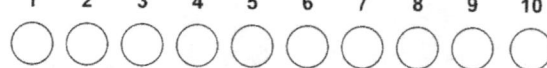

I view food as a way to honor God by caring for the body He's given me.

Subtotal (Add 1-10 for each): ____ / 50

Section 3: Exercise and General Healthiness

I engage in physical activity (walking, stretching, sports, etc.) at least three times a week.

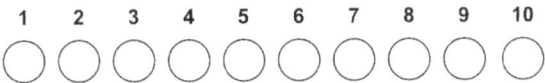

I feel physically strong and capable of meeting daily ministry demands.

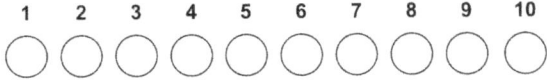

I attend regular medical check-ups and address health concerns promptly.

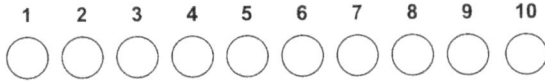

I manage stress through healthy outlets such as movement, hobbies, or outdoor time.

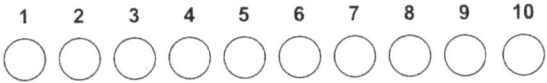

I view caring for my physical health as part of my calling to sustainable ministry.

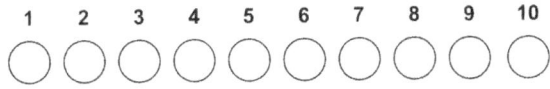

Subtotal (Add 1–10 for each): _____ / 50

Section 4: Need for Deep Friendships

I have one or more close friends with whom I can be completely honest.

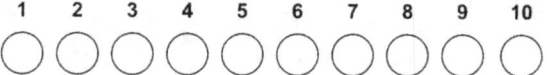

I regularly spend time with friends outside of ministry responsibilities.

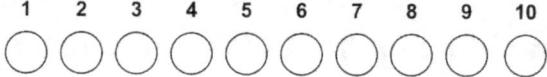

I feel emotionally supported by people who truly know me.

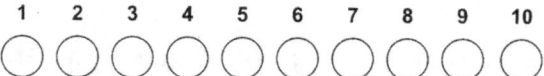

I do not feel isolated or alone in my leadership role.

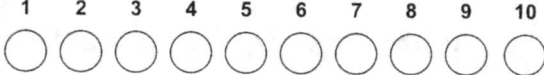

I intentionally invest in relationships that bring joy, laughter, and renewal.

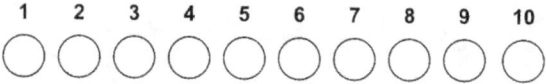

Subtotal (Add 1–10 for each): ____ / 50

Section 5: Sabbath and Spiritual Renewal

I practice a weekly Sabbath or day of rest, free from ministry work.

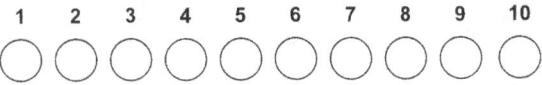

I take regular time for personal prayer, Scripture reflection, and silence before God.

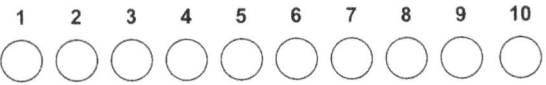

I engage in practices that nourish my soul (e.g., solitude, nature, worship).

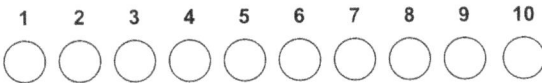

I maintain healthy boundaries between work/ministry and personal life.

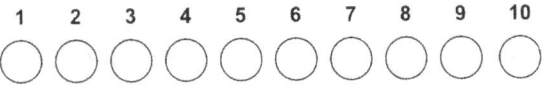

I sense that I am being spiritually renewed, not merely pouring out for others.

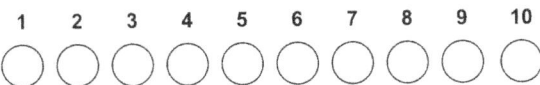

Subtotal (Add 1-10 for each): ____ / 50

Add all section scores for a total out of 250 points.

BURNOUT RISK LEVELS

250-200	Healthy & Sustanable: You're maintaining strong rhythms of physical and spiritual health. Keep protecting these boundaries
199-150	Caution Zone: Some key areas are weakening—review your lowest section and make small, intentional changes.
149-100	At Risk: Signs of burnout are emerging. Prioritize rest, health, and support systems immediately.
Less than 100	Critical: You may be experiencing significant burnout. Seek pastoral, medical. or counseling support to recover and rebuild balance.

STEP 2
PRAY AND CHANGE

1. Rest: What patterns of sleep or overwork need correction in your weekly rhythm? How consistent are you in maintaining healthy sleep patterns?

2. Nutrition: How can you better fuel your body as an act of stewardship? What changes can you make to your diet to honor your body as the temple of the Holy Spirit?

3. Exercise: What consistent physical activity could help sustain your ministry energy and focus? How do you integrate exercise into your weekly rhythm of ministry?

THE PHYSICAL NEEDS OF THE PASTOR

4. Friendship: Who in your life knows your heart beyond your title or role? How can you cultivate deeper trust? Do you have deep friendships that challenge and support your faith journey?

5.Sabbath: What would a regular rhythm of rest and renewal look like for you and your family? How might you cultivate a healthier Sabbath rhythm this month?

6. Integration: Which of these five areas needs the most immediate attention, and what step will you take this week to address it?

THE MAIN POINT

Only healthy pastors can live out their call for the long-term.

The stewardship of your physical well-being is not optional. Our ability to serve God-term cannot be disconnected from our physical well-being. Taking care of your body is a necessary part of your personal worship and commitment to God.

Additional Notes

Phillip G Andrade
PHOTOGRAPHY

"...do you not know that your body is a sanctuary of the Holy Spirit who is in you, whom you have from God, and that you are not your own? For you were bought with a price: therefore glorify God in your body."

1 Corinthians 6:19–20

THE SPIRITUAL NEEDS
OF THE PASTOR

03

THE SPIRITUAL NEEDS
OF THE PASTOR

Be on guard for yourselves and for all the flock, among which the Holy Spirit has made you overseers, to shepherd the church of God which He purchased with His own blood. Acts 20:28

Before Paul urged pastors to watch over the flock, he first commanded them to watch over themselves. A leader's spiritual vitality directly shapes the health of the church they lead. Ministry is not sustained by talent or technique but by a close intimate relationship with Jesus.

This chapter explores four vital areas of spiritual formation for leaders: Continued Learning, Personal Worship, Accountability, and Spiritual Gifts. Each of these are essential for sustaining a ministry that is authentic, enduring and deeply relational.

THE NEED FOR CONTINUED LEARNING

Be diligent to present yourself approved to God as a workman who does not need to be ashamed, accurately handling the word of truth.
2 Timothy 2:15

The call to ministry is also a call to lifelong learning. Those twin calls are inseparable. A pastor who stops growing in knowledge and application of the Scriptures will soon run dry in both conviction and content. The deeper we go into God's Word and its practical application into our lives, the deeper our own transformation becomes—and only then can we faithfully teach and

51

shepherd others. The pastor must serve out of a transformed life showing the power of the gospel and not just through skilled public speaking and a charismatic personality.

Paul told the Corinthians,

Be imitators of me, just as I also am of Christ. 1 Cor 11:1

Paul speaks this command not from his position of an apostle but because he was confident in his ongoing spiritual formation in Christ. Pastors cannot lead others where they themselves are unwilling to go. Many complain about the struggles of pastoral ministry. I won't argue with that claim. Leading a church can be one of the most difficult calls to follow. Yet, why do we rarely talk about the abundant blessings we have in that call as well?

If you are a pastor your church pays you to study and grow in Christ. What a blessing and privilege it is to receive such a gift. So let's endeavor to take that gift and do well with it for the sake of our people and the glory of Jesus.

Ongoing learning involves more than sermon preparation.

• It means reading the Scriptures devotionally and studying them for personal growth before professional use.

• It means pursuing continuing education, theological seminars, leadership conferences, or spiritual retreats that keep our minds sharp and informed.

• It means reading books in other disciplines besides the Bible to have a handle on many subjects so we can bring biblical truth to bear on every aspect of the world views that are out there and to make sure the world view we have is truly biblical.

• It means Scripture memorization. Many Christians tend to do this when they are younger in the faith. My experience is that this discipline tends to drop off the more we gain a greater understanding of the Bible and redemptive history. That is, we rest on our general knowledge to the neglect of internalizing important Scriptures.

PRINCIPLES OF CONTINUED LEARNING EXERCISE

The Scriptures are replete with calls to continue in learning. As a short exercise, what do these Scriptures tell us about the importance of this topic? Summarize the principle and write down one step you can take in growing toward the principle. Focus on the verse listed but also look at the greater context for more understanding.

Let the wise man hear and increase in learning, And a man of understanding will acquire guidance, Proverbs 1:5

PRINCIPLE:

FIRST STEP:

THE SPIRITUAL NEEDS OF THE PASTOR

For this reason also, since the day we heard, we have not ceased to pray for you and to ask that you may be filled with the full knowledge of His will in all spiritual wisdom and understanding, so that you may walk in a manner worthy of the Lord, to please Him in all respects, bearing fruit in every good work and multiplying in the full knowledge of God; being strengthened with all power, according to His glorious might, for the attaining of all steadfastness and patience; joyously giving thanks to the Father, who has qualified us to share in the inheritance of the saints in light. Colossians 1:9–12

PRINCIPLE:

FIRST STEP:

You therefore, beloved, knowing this beforehand, be on your guard lest you, having been carried away by the error of unprincipled men, fall from your own steadfastness, but grow in the grace and knowledge of our Lord and Savior Jesus Christ. To Him be the glory, both now and to the day of eternity. Amen.. 2 Peter 3:17-18

PRINCIPLE:

FIRST STEP:

THE SPIRITUAL NEEDS OF THE PASTOR

It is important to immediately apply these things to your life. In the space below write down three practical steps you can implement in your continuing learning. For example: "I will read three biographies this year," "I will research a local seminar and schedule the time to go this fall."

1.

2.

3.

THE NEED FOR PERSONAL WORSHIP

Come, let us worship and bow down, Let us kneel before Yahweh our Maker. Psalm 95:6

Pastors are often professional worshipers—constantly leading others in praise, prayer, and preaching. Yet this professional role can unintentionally replace personal devotion. It is possible to become so familiar with the mechanics of worship that we forget the intimacy with God it brings to us outside of the role as pastor.

When ministry becomes routine, worship can turn transactional—something we do for God rather than a time to be simply be with God. We plan services, write sermons, or choose worship music and organize the service order, yet rarely linger privately in the presence of Jesus.

This is so essential but often overlooked. Our congregants believe we are so blessed because we get to "spend all our time with Jesus." While they are correct; that would be a blessing, in practicality it is a blessing often not realized.

I experienced this firsthand during my recent sabbatical. For 40 years I've been in the mode of professional minister of some sort, whether it be a youth master, missionary on the field, or Pastor. Of course, there have been times in those 40 years where my connection to Jesus was sweet and wonderful. But if I'm honest for many of those years, my relationship with Jesus has been one of professional relationship and not child of God. Over the last few years, I've been very aware of the times I've been away on vacation and attended church someplace else. I so wanted to worship Jesus as just me, Phil, yet I found that during worship, my mind would wander, and I would fall into professional mode thinking to myself, "I would've preached that differently," or "that worship song was really good. We should use that in our church services," or even judgmentally, "that wasn't a very good sermon. He didn't even touch on the most important parts of that passage." I did not want to respond like that to worship. My heart's desire was that I would connect with Jesus and sense his love for me; that I would experience his glory and his Spirit working in and through me. Getting out of the professional mode was so difficult. Then came the three-month sabbatical.

The first few times I attended worship in a different church. I went through that same pattern in my mind. It was wandering to the professional aspects of what I was experiencing. It wasn't long, however, probably because I didn't have any agenda to fulfill or any deadlines to meet. When I began to shed the shift to thinking professionally, then I actually began to worship. Not as Pastor Phil, but as Phil. Renewing and remembering his goodness to me when he saved me from my sin, guilt and brokenness. I sensed my dry spirituality, leaving in a renewed sense of Thanksgiving and worship of the holy one being realized in my life. Lest I'm confusing you, I don't mean to say that I hadn't felt God's power and presence in my life up to this point. I often felt his power and presence as I ministered or preached or shared the gospel. I have been blessed with seeing God work through me in those very areas where I am weak and unable. But in the area of personal connection in worship, something had come alive again.

Every now and again this thought runs through my head, "If the church didn't pay me to be here would I even show up every weekend?" Yeah, it's a horrible thought but it's probably in your head every now and then too. Something has changed, though for me because when I got back and started worshiping again with my congregation, I had developed the skill set, if I can call it that, to let everything go, and just focus on the Lord. Now rather than asking that horrible question, the question I ask is "how can anyone who understands the grace of Jesus not have the passion to come worship him as often as they can? What can be more important to do on a Sunday than gather together with God's people and worship?"

There is a stark difference between those two questions and the motivation behind them. What changed in my life was a proactive decision to seek him out beyond the professional role I have been called to. As pastors we have to find a way to be both professional how we fulfill our role and authentic and passionate about our individual relationship with Jesus. We cannot have a long-term sustainable ministry if we don't learn to balance both those things.

I don't have all the answers, and every now and then I find myself falling into the same rut. I was in before, but I am determined to have greater balance in this area. There is nothing more important than being the person I was created to be. I was created to be first and foremost, and you were too, a worshiper.

Personal worship is essential to maintaining a heart for God. All the Bible study, parsing Greek verbs, books written won't matter much if we do those things outside a vital relationship with our Savior. We must be proactive because it won't happen all by itself. It might mean planning time alone in the woods, playing an instrument in solitude, journaling our thoughts, prayers and heartaches, whatever it takes. Remember, Jesus Himself modeled this need for times alone with God.

And in the early morning, while it was still dark, Jesus rose up, went out of the house, and went away to a desolate place, and was praying there. Mark 1:35

But He Himself would often slip away to the desolate regions and pray. Luke 5:16

Two words should jump out from those passages: often and solitary. Jesus needed to be alone with God often. In some way, solitary places almost become a symbol of the way Jesus dealt with the threat of being alone. When he was feeling alone because of the demands of ministry, disappointment, and grief, he chose, often, to be alone with the Father. When we are feeling abandoned, overwhelmed, stressed out even on the verge of burnout, our first response should be to go to a solitary place and worship. We must learn to step out of the proverbial pulpit and bow before the one who loves us. Our ministries must flow from intimacy with God.

Start by adding these Scriptures to memory if you haven't already

God is spirit, and those who worship Him
must worship in spirit and truth." John 4:24

O God, You are my God; I shall seek You earnestly; My soul thirsts for
You, my flesh yearns for You, In a dry and weary land without water.
Thus I have beheld You in the sanctuary, To see Your power and Your
glory. Because Your lovingkindness is better than life, My lips will laud
You. Thus I will bless You as long as I live; I will lift up my hands in
Your name. Psalm 63:1-4

Martha, Martha, you are worried and bothered about so many things,
but only one thing is necessary, for Mary has chosen the good part,..
Luke 10:41–42a

THE NEED FOR ACCOUNTABILITY

Iron sharpens iron, So one man sharpens another." Proverbs 27:17

Isolation is one of the greatest dangers in pastoral ministry. Many pastors serve for years without a single trusted friend or mentor who they can be honest with. This lack of accountability leaves leaders vulnerable to moral failure, emotional and spiritual collapse, spiritual pride and the manipulation of God's people.

The New Testament presents a different pattern. Paul never ministered alone—he worked with Barnabas, Silas, Timothy, Luke, and others. We even get this story in Galatians where Paul holds Peter accountable when his actions contradicted the gospel (Galatians 2:11–14). Accountability was part of apostolic life. How much more is it needed now when new challenges from western culture and affluence invade our world.

In 2015, 37% of pastors reported getting some sort of spiritual support from a mentor or accountability partner several times a month. In the more recent data, that has dropped to 22%.[1] In that same report, Barna notes that "pastors are not often receiving spiritual support from a mentor or a network of peers."[2] A study from the Pastoral Care Institute (2017) revealed that 40% of pastors lacked accountability often associated with feelings of isolation.[3] Other studies in some areas show things may be looking up. Thom Rainer's research on church leadership found that 72% of pastors in larger churches participated in some form of peer accountability, but this wasn't always the same as formal mentorship.[4]

This research didn't review the situation in smaller churches where the resources for effective church accountability structures may be more difficult to maintain. In short, there is not a lot of clear research in this area. My instincts tell me that if I, as a pastor, have difficulty in getting church members to embrace mentorship or any form of accountability partnerships then the frequency among pastors may be just, if not more, rampant. This is unfortunate because healthy accountability can provide so much to keep a pastor healthy physically, mentally and spiritually.

Study the following Scriptures and briefly record what characteristic would be beneficial in a mentoring/accountability relationship.

Brothers, even if anyone is caught in any transgression, you who are spiritual, restore such a one in a spirit of gentleness, each of you looking to yourself, so that you too will not be tempted. Bear one another's burdens, and so fulfill the law of Christ. Gal 6:1-2

[1] Barna Group. "Pastor Support Systems." Barna Research. Accessed December 28, 2025. https://www.barna.com/research/pastor-support-systems/.
[2] Ibid.
[3] Pastoral Care Institute. The Isolation of Ministry. 2017.
[4] Rainer, Thom. The State of Pastoral Leadership. 2019.

Therefore, confess your sins to one another, and pray for one another so that you may be healed. The effective prayer of a righteous man can accomplish much. Jms 5:16

Therefore, comfort one another and build up one another, just as you also are doing..1 Thess 5:11

All Scripture is God-breathed and profitable for teaching, for reproof, for correction, for training in righteousness, so that the man of God may be equipped, having been thoroughly equipped for every good work. 2 Tim 3:16-17

THE SPIRITUAL NEEDS OF THE PASTOR

Let the word of Christ dwell in you richly, with all wisdom teaching and admonishing one another with psalms and hymns and spiritual songs, singing with gratefulness in your hearts to God. Col 3:16

But I myself am also convinced about you, my brothers, that you yourselves are full of goodness, having been filled with all knowledge and being able also to admonish one another. Rom 15:14

Biblical Counseling Coalition has a good and succinct article on what is needed to have enduring accountability relationships. This is a good starting point to get something started in your life.[5]

Healthy accountability includes honest dialogue about our whole person. It would include being challenged in every area of our growth – physical, spiritual, and emotional. It delves into the seldom practiced arts of confession, correction and encouragement. A biblical accountability partnership is never about controlling one another it is about truly caring for someone at their basic needs. Accountability seeks to protect both the leaders and the people he serves. Without accountability, you will drift into isolation and potential danger.

---

[5] Biblical Counseling Coalition. "Seven Marks of Enduring Accountability Relationships." Biblical Counseling Coalition. March 23, 2016. Accessed December 28, 2025. https://www.biblicalcounselingcoalition.org/2016/03/23/seven-marks-of-enduring-accountability-relationships/.

THE NEED TO FOCUS ON SPIRITUAL GIFTS

But to each one is given the manifestation of the Spirit for what is profitable. 1 Corinthians 12:7

Many pastors I have spoken to often convey that they feel pulled in 100 directions at once. They preach, teach and counsel. They pray, study and worship. They make sure the building is locked, clean the toilets, and pick up the mess left out in the church entry way. They do the bulletin when the secretary is sick, they handle the youth meeting when the staff is late, and they are expected to fill in the gaps wherever they appear. Sadly, much of their time is spent majoring in the minors.

The Scriptures emphatically teach that every pastor has been uniquely gifted by the Holy Spirit for ministry. They have not been given every spiritual gift but like other Christians they have been given some. Yet many leaders spend most of their time on tasks that drain rather than energize them. They find themselves focusing on everything else except in the areas that they have been gifted in. The result is frustration, burnout, and diminished fruitfulness.

Paul's teaching in 1 Corinthians 12 reminds us that the body of Christ thrives when each part functions in its proper place. When pastors neglect their God-given gifts to meet every secondary demand, the whole body suffers. While leadership requires flexibility and humility, it also demands discernment. Pastors must learn to delegate, equip others (Ephesians 4:11–12), and focus primarily on the areas where the Spirit has gifted them. A leader constantly functioning outside of their gifts will eventually collapse. Understand this: Doing everything is not faithfulness. I fall into this false belief all too often. My thinking goes like this:

"That person is not pulling their weight in planning worship like they committed to. So, I must jump in and do their job because we should do everything excellent for Jesus and I cannot let the service be second rate." "For some reason the church bathrooms were not cleaned this week, and we have a conference this afternoon, so I need to go over there and clean them up (and miss time with my family)."

We will talk about this thought process later when we discuss responsibilities in Chapter 3. For now, we need to stop equating busyness and picking up the pieces and therefore neglecting the primacy of our gifts and calling it faithfulness. It is the opposite. It probably is enablement and unfaithfulness to the call to build up others and focus our time to do the things God called

THE SPIRITUAL NEEDS OF THE PASTOR

us to do.

A study by Lifeway found that 51% of pastors say they need to focus more on managing their time and avoiding over-commitment. Though not much study has been done on how the allocation of time relates to spiritual gifts versus other tasks, this study strongly suggests that pastors who are struggling with time management may not be able to concentrate solely on gift-aligned ministry[6]

As each one has received a gift, employ it in serving one another as good stewards of the manifold grace of God
1 Peter 4:10

Trust me, I know it feels ungodly to let some things slide. It can feel like you are letting Jesus down. Peter says here that we are stewards of the gifts we have received. So I encourage you to be a faithful steward and refocus how you spend your time to maximize the fruit from your gifts trusting Him to provide that which human effort cannot.

[6] Lifeway Research. "Pastors Report Struggling with Time Management, Over-Commitment." Lifeway Research. April 12, 2022. Accessed December 28, 2025. https://research.lifeway.com/2022/04/12/pastors-report-struggling-with-time-management-over-commitment/.

PRINCIPLES

1 **Continued Learning** : Leaders must continually grow to lead a growing church. Leaders set the tone in their congregations for spiritual growth.

2 **Personal Worship**: Ministry flows from intimacy with Jesus, not performance for Jesus.

3 **Accountability**: Isolation can lead to many types of failures. Accountability brings safety

4 **Spiritual Gifts**: Faithfulness means serving primarily within God's ministry gifts.

REFLECTION

And He Himself gave some as apostles, and some as prophets, and some as evangelists, and some as pastors and teachers, for the equipping of the saints for the work of service, to the building up of the body of Christ, Ephesians 4:11-12

Consider the Scripture above and interact with the following statement:

Leaders should not only develop their own gifts but also empower others to use theirs, building a stronger and more balanced body.

In what ways have you seen the use or lack of use of your spiritual gifts directly impact your call to build up others?

Write down a next step plan for each question below. Don't answer in a nebulous theoretical way. Make the steps practical and measurable.

Ongoing Learning: What steps are you taking to deepen your understanding of Scripture apart from sermon preparation? That is, how can you pursue ongoing learning beyond sermon preparation?

Personal Worship: When was the last time you worshiped God apart from your role as a leader? How can you create 'sacred space' each week for worship that is personal, not professional?

Accountability: Who has permission to ask you hard questions about your soul, habits, and integrity? Do you have a structure for accountability and mentoring relationships?

Spiritual Gifts: Are you spending more time in areas of giftedness or areas of frustration? How can you adjust your ministry focus? Would you say you are primarily serving within the areas of your spiritual gifts?

Integration: Which of these four areas needs the most work in your life right now? What is the first practical step you will take this week?

THE MAIN POINT.

IT TAKES A SPIRITUALLY HEALTHY LEADER TO SHAPE A SPIRITUALLY HEALTHY CHURCH. AS LEADERSHIP GOES SO DOES THE CHURCH.

Phillip G Andrade
PHOTOGRAPHY

Be on guard for yourselves and for all the flock, among which the Holy Spirit has made you overseers..."

Acts 20:28a

THE MENTAL NEEDS
OF THE PASTOR

04
THE MENTAL NEEDS
OF THE PASTOR

Guard your heart with all diligence, For from it flow the springs of life.
Proverbs 4:23

A pastor will quickly fall if he attempts to lead solely from his skill set and professional training. Leaders must lead from the inside out. That is, our interior world of thoughts and emotions will influence how we lead through our skills and training. It is in our minds, our inner life, where truth is processed, burdens are carried, traumas are buried and temptations are entertained.

The pathway from our inner thoughts to our outer actions, though it may not be apparent, forms a direct connection. Therefore, mental health is not a supplement for church leaders—it is an imperative. I am not saying that we have to have it all together in everyway. We all struggle with a variety of issues that may relate to our mental health. The danger here is that we ignore the signs or try to normalize them. If we are suffering from depression, for example, it is not wise to ignore it and hope it goes away nor is it wise to shrug it off and say, "well everyone struggles with depression now and then so it is no big deal." We must mind our mental health and bring it under the authority of Jesus seeking healing in these areas whether it is through gaining coping skills or direct medical intervention if warranted.

Many pastors enter ministry with the worthy goal of serving God by serving others but all to often neglect their own mental health. The pressures of leadership, criticism, loneliness, and unrelenting impossible expectations can distort thought patterns, create anxiety, feed our dysfunctions and ultimately affect the depth of our relationship with Jesus and with others.

According to recent studies data consistently shows 1 in 4 pastors struggle with mental illness, usually with anxiety and depression as top concerns. Sadly, younger pastors (18-44) report higher rates. Not surprisingly, stress affects 63% of pastors.[1] 75% feel "extremely/highly stressed.[2]" In another study, once again, 75% of pastors reported feeling "extremely stressed" or "highly stressed.[3]"

This trend of pastors who struggle with mental health issues is not diminishing. Many pastors I've talked to have seen a sharp rise in mental health cases post-covid in their congregations. It should be no surprise that the trend finds its way to church leadership.

In this chapter, we will explore three vital areas for maintaining a healthy mind in ministry. Once again, this chapter is not meant to be comprehensive, but a starting point for continued growth and personal exploration.

MENTAL HEALTH IN PASTORAL LEADERSHIP

26% of Pastors report struggling with some type of mental illness.

37% Pastors under 45 who have struggled with mental illness.

75% of Pastors report they are "extremely stressed" or "highly stressed."

- Understanding the Dark Side of Leadership

- Practicing Times of Renewal

- Balancing Our Responsibilities

[1] Lifeway Research. "Stress Tops Mental Challenges Pastors Face." Lifeway Research. April 26, 2022. Accessed December 28, 2025. https://research.lifeway.com/2022/04/26/stress-tops-mental-challenges-pastors-face/.
[2] Ibid.
[3] Soul Shepherding. "Pastors Under Stress." Soul Shepherding. Accessed December 28, 2025. https://www.soulshepherding.org/pastors-under-stress/.

UNDERSTANDING THE DARK SIDE OF LEADERSHIP

*If we say that we have no sin, we deceive ourselves
and the truth is not in us. 1 John 1:8*

Every leader carries within themselves a combination of divine potential and human brokenness. Sam Rima, in his book Overcoming the Dark Side of Leadership,[4] asserts that "When leaders fail to recognize and deal with their own dark side, it will eventually control them, and they will become a liability to themselves, their followers, and their organizations."

The "dark side" refers to those messy areas of the soul—unhealed wounds, unmet needs, pride, insecurity, fear, or control—that shape how we lead. When left alone and not 'redeemed' by the Spirit, these dysfunctions can manifest in ministry as perfectionism, manipulation, isolation, burnout and a host of other dysfunctions. Understanding your dark side is not about self-condemnation but about self-awareness that the dark side exists and by God's grace it can be redeemed.

Obviously, there is no Scripture that uses the term "dark side," but clearly, we are called to look inward. David prayed,

*Search me, O God, and know my heart; Try me and know my anxious
thoughts; And see if there be any hurtful way in me, And lead me in the
everlasting way. Ps 139:23–24*

It is also worth noting that Paul was well aware of his weaknesses. He writes about the transformative power of Jesus to flow through his weaknesses.

*"My grace is sufficient for you, for power is perfected in weakness."
Most gladly, therefore, I will rather boast in my weaknesses, so that the
power of Christ may dwell in me. 2 Cor 12:9*

Healthy leadership begins with the humility to let God reveal what drives us and to bring our inner dysfunctions into the light of His truth. Clearly stated: Awareness is the beginning of transformation. If a leader is unaware of their dysfunctions and how they can affect ministry, then the leader's ministry will be shaped by those very dysfunctions.

---

[4] McIntosh, Gary L., and Samuel D. Rima Sr. Overcoming the Dark Side of Leadership. Grand Rapids: Baker, 2007. 21-22.

THE MENTAL NEEDS OF THE PASTOR

STEP 1
WRESTLE WITH THE SCRIPTURE

What does the following passage say about what drives us? How does that relate to our dark side personality dysfunctions such as co-dependency, paranoia, passive-aggressivity, narcissism and compulsiveness?

But I say, walk by the Spirit and you will not carry out the desire of the flesh. For the flesh sets its desire against the Spirit, and the Spirit against the flesh; for these are in opposition to one another, so that you do not do the things that you want. Gal 5:16–17

STEP 2
ADVANCED LEARNING

Purchase the book referenced above - Overcoming the Dark Side of Leadership. Read and take the enclosed assessment. Create a plan to take the appropriate steps to understand, discover and redeem your dark side shape. Share your discoveries with a trusted friend or colleague.

[ ] I've ordered the book.

[ ] I've read and taken the assessments.

[ ] I've made a plan for change.

[ ] I've made a plan to share.

Healthy pastors are not those who have no dark side (every human has one) but those who have learned to recognize it, confront it, and allow Christ to redeem it.

PRACTICING TIMES OF RENEWAL

Do not be conformed to this world, but be transformed by the renewing of your mind, so that you may approve what the will of God is, that which is good and pleasing and perfect. Romans 12:2

What is the difference between renewal and sabbath? Though there is some overlap the difference is that renewal is more of an intentional practice of stepping away from the pressures of ministry to refocus the mind and restore perspective. While Sabbath emphasizes rest and rhythm, renewal focuses specifically on mental and emotional recalibration.

The pressures of ministry can easily trap leaders in cycles of mental exhaustion. At one point in my first senior pastorate, I wasn't a year into ministry before exhaustion hit. While still settling into a normal pattern of ministry (as normal as one can be I suppose) a string of tragedies struck my church, my family and I was reeling. A key couple in my church were in a car accident and spent weeks in the hospital until the husband died, shortly followed by his wife. Not long after the funerals, my mother passed away and two months later my wife's father suddenly passed away. The month hadn't ended before a young man who was the church drummer took his own life. I was physically, emotionally, spiritually and mentally exhausted. I was ready to quit before I had even really started. Thankfully, my denomination at the time recognized the condition we were in and promptly provided a retreat for us to get away and process the situation with other pastors and missionaries in similar times of struggle. Of course that was a unique set of circumstances we were dealing with but the same mental exhaustion can build up over longer periods of time with the constant output—preaching, counseling, leading, solving. All these demands tell us to give our all, but we must also allow time for God to fill us when we empty out. Notice I said that we must allow time. This will not happen on its own because our default is go go go, not "Be still, and know that I am God; Ps 46:10

This type of renewal demands we develop several practices in the following areas:

- **Healthy relationships** — Being proactive in spending time with those who fill your soul rather than drain it.

- **Healthy thought practices** — Replacing anxiety and self-criticism with gratitude and focus on God's Word.[5]

- **Healthy space** — Stepping away for retreats, devotional reading, experiencing the arts, and spending time in nature or silence.

Even Jesus practiced this type of renewal. He spent time with his friends. He often refocused on his call when those around him criticized and jeered. He even withdrew from people even though the needs around him were great.

> *He withdrew from there in a boat to a desolate place by Himself." Mt 14:13*

For the workaholics out there, renewal is not avoidance of responsibilities—it is obedience to the principle that ministry without renewal leads to burnout. It is recognizing that we can do nothing of spiritual significance without reliance on him.

> *I am the vine, you are the branches; he who abides in Me and I in him, he bears much fruit, for apart from Me you can do nothing. John 15:5*

---

[5] To clarify, some mental health issues such as some types of anxiety, etc. can't be healed by reading the Bible more or other spiritual disciplines. Some issues are physically based and trained doctors should be consulted. The focus here is not on chronic issues but rather on those issues that are spiritual in nature that Paul encourages us to renew in our minds.

STEP 1
MAKE A PLAN

For the following Scriptures, write down one practical and measurable step you can take to refining the practice of renewal in your life. Remember, renewal must be intentional. It requires planning, boundaries, and the humility to admit that even pastors need replenishment.

Therefore I exhort you, brothers, by the mercies of God, to present your bodies as a sacrifice—living, holy, and pleasing to God, which is your spiritual service of worship. And do not be conformed to this world, but be transformed by the renewing of your mind, so that you may approve what the will of God is, that which is good and pleasing and perfect.
Romans 12:1-2

Be anxious for nothing, but in everything by prayer and petition with thanksgiving let your requests be made known to God. And the peace of God, which surpasses all comprehension, will guard your hearts and your minds in Christ Jesus. Finally, brothers, whatever is true, whatever is dignified, whatever is right, whatever is pure, whatever is lovely, whatever is commendable, if there is any excellence and if anything worthy of praise, consider these things. Philippians 4:6-8

THE MENTAL NEEDS OF THE PASTOR

The steadfast of mind You will keep in perfect peace
Because he trusts in You. Isaiah 26:3

BALANCING OUR RESPONSIBILITIES

I planted, Apollos watered, but God was causing the growth.
1 Corinthians 3:6

One of the greatest mental burdens pastors face is the confusion of responsibility. I've seen it in every kind of church, but I've mostly seen it in my life. I can definitively say that every time I was heading towards burnout one of the primary factors was that I was overwhelmed by responsibilities that were not mine. Much of my mental energy was spent of trying to deal with responsibilities that were never assigned to me which lead to the neglect of those responsibilities that were mine. So, I found myself spending time and energy on the very things that would never bring fruit. How frustrating and harmful it was. Let me break it down a bit.

Ministry demands much from us, but not everything that demands our attention is truly ours to carry. Paul reminds us that God gives the growth. How often do you and I 'try to make things happen?' Understanding the principle of how God grows things brings profound mental freedom.

There are three basic categories of responsibility in ministry. Things that are

- **My Responsibility** – to study, pray, preach faithfully, shepherd wisely, and live with integrity etc.

- **Others' Responsibility** – their spiritual growth, obedience, and maturity of those we serve.

- **God's Responsibility** – Transformation, conviction, and fruit of the ministry.

Pastors often blur these lines. We try to carry others' spiritual growth, their obedience, their healing, or even their salvation. When people resist spiritual growth, leaders often internalize failure: "Why didn't they listen? What did I do wrong?" This misplaced burden leads to guilt, frustration, and exhaustion and eventually burnout.

Christopher Ash says that *"There is a difference between godly sacrifice and needless burnout.[6]"* Ash later recounts a pastor's letter that equates this tendency to *"a form of heroic suicide.[7]"* Healthy ministry requires learning to stay in our lane.

We plant and water, but only God causes growth. When we take on the responsibilities of others it is not the loving thing to do though it seems like it is. We want them to grow, for example, so we will try to force it by guilt or some other means that probably borders on manipulation. This takes away from their personal responsibility. When we take on God's responsibility in their lives for bringing growth it is simply idolatry of self. As leaders our primary ministry is to plant and water. Wayne Cordeiro writes

> *"Wrongly, we try to position ourselves as the person to run to for help, when all along we need to be pointing people to Christ. It may sound strange, but there is a sense in which I can truthfully say that the church does not exist to help people, to solve their problems and alleviate their disappointments... The primary reason the church exists is to worship God and to point people to Christ, the ultimate solution to their problems.[8]"*

How much pressure do we bring on ourselves and our families when we take on the responsibility to help everyone when that is beyond our reach. We point people to Jesus. This perspective guards our mental and emotional health, keeping us grounded in grace rather than trapped in performance.

[6] Ash, Christopher. Zeal and Burnout. The Good Book Company, 2016. 24.
[7] Ibid. 25
[8] Cordeiro, Wayne. Sifted. Grand Rapids: Zondervan, 2012. 63.

STEP 1

WRESTLE WITH THE SCRIPTURE

Read each Scripture then rewrite the main point from each as a prayer to God that he would imprint the principal into your life.

What then is Apollos? And what is Paul? Servants through whom you believed, even as the Lord gave to each one. I planted, Apollos watered, but God was causing the growth. So then neither the one who plants nor the one who waters is anything, but God who causes the growth. Now he who plants and he who waters are one, but each will receive his own reward according to his own labor. For we are God's fellow workers; you are God's field, God's building. 1 Corinthians 3:5–9

But each one must examine his own work, and then he will have reason for boasting in regard to himself alone, and not in regard to another. For each one will bear his own load. Galatians 6:4-5

"Come to Me, all who are weary and heavy-laden, and I will give you rest. Take My yoke upon you and learn from Me, for I am gentle and humble in heart, and you will find rest for your souls. For My yoke is easy and My burden is light." Matthew 11:28–30

PRINCIPLES

1 **Understand Your Darkside:** Awareness of your core dysfunctions leads to transformation.

2 **Practice Renewal:** Ministry without renewal leads to burnout.

3 **Balance Responsibilities:** Point people to Jesus—God gives the growth.

PASTORAL BURNOUT & MINISTRY CRISIS ASSESSMENT TOOL

Instructions: Rate each statement on a scale of 1–5 based on how true it is for you over the past 3–6 months.

1 = Almost never / Strongly disagree

2 = Rarely

3 = Sometimes

4 = Often

5 = Almost always / Strongly agree

Emotional & Spiritual Vitality (1–10)

I feel emotionally drained by the end of most ministry days.

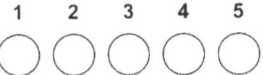

My prayer life feels dry, forced, or non-existent.

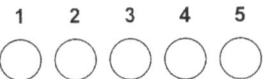

I experience regular cynicism about the church or people I serve.

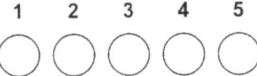

I feel guilty when I'm not working on something ministry-related.

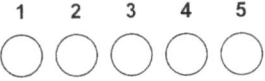

I resent people who ask for my time or help.

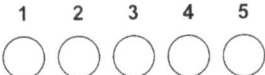

I have lost the joy I once had in ministry.

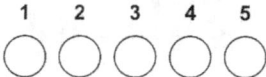

I feel distant from God even when I'm doing "spiritual" activities.

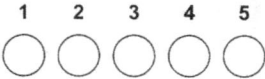

I preach or lead out of duty rather than genuine passion.

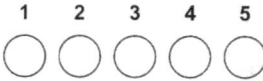

I secretly wonder if God has abandoned me or if I've failed Him.

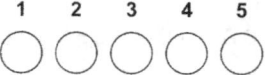

I struggle to experience genuine compassion for hurting people.

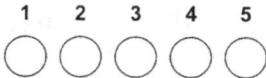

Physical & Energy Levels (11–18)

I am chronically fatigued, even after a full night's sleep.

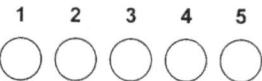

I experience frequent headaches, muscle tension, or stomach issues.

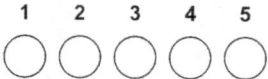

My sleep is restless or interrupted by ministry thoughts.

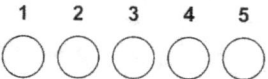

I feel that I cannot take one more meeting.

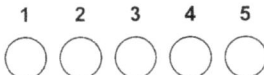

I have gained or lost significant weight without trying.

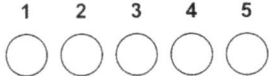

I rarely feel fully rested, even on days off.

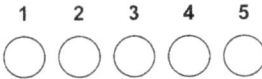

Minor illnesses seem to linger longer than they used to.

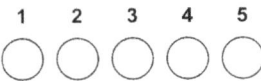

I have little energy left for my family or personal hobbies.

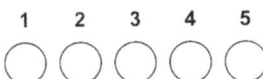

Boundaries & Work Habits (19–28)

I say "yes" to most requests even when I'm already overloaded.

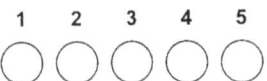

I work more than 50 hours a week on average.

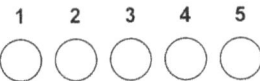

My day off is regularly interrupted by ministry demands.

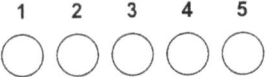

THE MENTAL NEEDS OF THE PASTOR

I check emails, texts, or social media about church matters constantly.

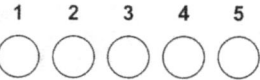

I feel I am the only one who can do certain tasks in the church.

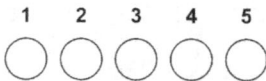

I cancel personal or family plans because of unexpected ministry needs (including dinners together or time with children).

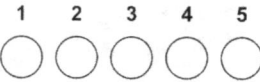

I have no consistent Sabbath practice (at least a full 24-hour break a week).

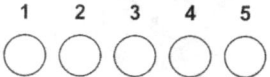

I bring work home emotionally even when I'm physically away.

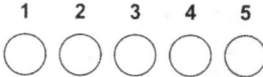

I struggle to delegate significant responsibilities to others.

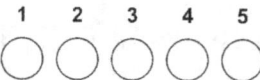

People close to me have expressed concern about my pace of life.

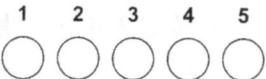

Relationships & Support (29–36)

I feel lonely in ministry; few people really know how I'm doing.

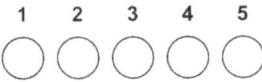

My spouse (if applicable) feels neglected or resentful of the church.

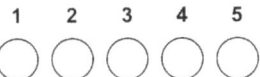

I avoid deep relationships because I don't have time or energy.

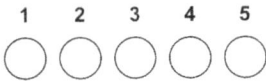

I have no close friend outside my church who can speak truth into my life.

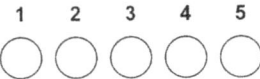

Conflict with church members leaves me anxious for days.

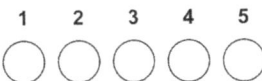

I fear letting people see my weaknesses or struggles.

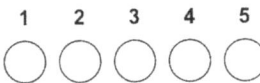

My children (if applicable) rarely get my full attention.

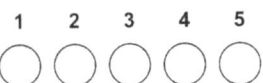

I have no mentor, coach, counselor, or peer group I meet with regularly.

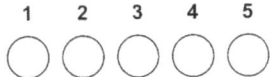

Identity & Self-Worth (37–44)

My sense of worth is tied to ministry productivity or people's approval.

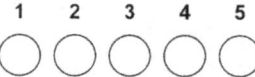

I feel like a failure when attendance, giving, or growth is down.

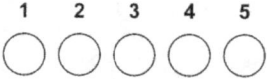

I compare myself constantly to other pastors or churches.

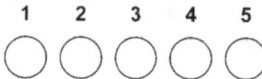

I secretly believe "If I don't do it, it won't get done right."

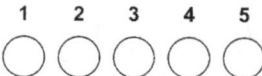

Criticism (even constructive) devastates me.

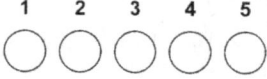

I struggle to receive compliments or celebrate successes.

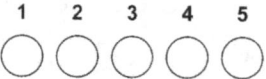

I feel trapped in ministry with no realistic way out.

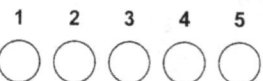

I fantasize about quitting ministry entirely.

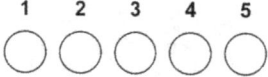

Hope & Future Orientation (45–50)

I dread Sundays or upcoming ministry events.

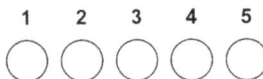

I can't remember the last time I felt genuine hope about the future.

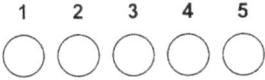

I have intrusive thoughts of escape (quitting, running away, etc.).

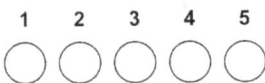

I use food, alcohol, pornography, shopping, or other escapes to cope.

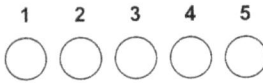

I have had thoughts that the church or my family would be better off without me.

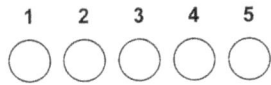

When I imagine the next 5 years in ministry, I feel despair rather than anticipation.

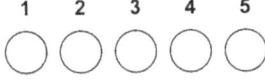

Scoring: Add up all 50 responses.

250-188

BURNOUT

In need of drastic steps. You are in a crisis state. Immediate intervention is essential (extended sabbatical, professional counseling, medical evaluation, possible interim leadership change).

187-150

DANGER STAGE

In need of immediate help. You are on the brink. Without swift, significant changes, full burnout is likely within months. Urgent action required (counseling, reduced load, accountability).

149-113

MOVING TOWARD BURNOUT

Warning signs are strong. You still have time to reverse the trajectory, but intentional changes in rhythm, support, and self-care are needed now.

112-76

LOW CHANCE OF BURNOUT

You are experiencing normal ministry stress, but protective factors are in place. Continue guarding your rhythms and relationships.

75-50

DOING GREAT

Good balance of ministry and life. You are sustaining a healthy, long-term rhythm. Keep protecting what is working and stay humble and vigilant.

NEXT STEPS

• Share your results with at least one trusted person (spouse, mentor, elder, counselor).

If you scored in one of the top three stages, consider...

• Schedule a medical check-up (burnout can affect us physically)

• Book an appointment with a counselor or pastor-specialized therapist.

• Discuss with your leadership about your personal ministry boundaries and support network.

REFLECTION

UNDERSTANDING YOUR DARK SIDE

What personal weaknesses or patterns have the potential to harm your ministry if left unchecked?

Who in your life helps you see what you cannot see about yourself?

Have you identified patterns of dysfunction that influence your leadership?

PRACTICING RENEWAL

When was the last time you intentionally stepped away from ministry to renew your mind and relationships?

What practices bring you mental peace and spiritual clarity?

What practices renew your mind and refresh your soul?

BALANCING RESPONSIBILITIES

Are there burdens you are carrying that rightly belong to others—or to God?

How can you remind yourself daily that ministry fruitfulness depends on God's grace, not your effort?

Where might you be taking on responsibilities that belong to others or to God?

INTEGRATION

Which of these three areas needs the most attention in your life today?

What small adjustment this week could move you toward mental and emotional health?

THE MAIN POINT

Our inner lives have a direct correlation to our outward ministries. If we do not allow for times of mental renewal we will have nothing left to give.

RHYTHMS OF REST AND RENEWAL

05

RHYTHMS OF REST AND RENEWAL

Be watchful, stand firm in the faith, act like men, be strong. Let all that you do be done in love. 1 Cor 16:13–14

Full time ministry is a study in extremes. It can be as emotionally demanding as it is spiritually fulfilling. Pastors rejoice at weddings and weep at funerals. They are entrusted with confidences, take on the pain of others, and often carry their own hidden wounds and scars. Emotional resilience—the ability to recover, adapt, and remain faithful in a world of extremes is a learned skill essential for long-term ministry.

Emotional resilience is the ability to respond to the demands of ministry with grace, endurance and patience. Jesus Himself experienced deep emotions—He wept at Lazarus's tomb (John 11:35), felt deep pain and abandonment in Gethsemane (Luke 22:44). He expressed righteous anger in the temple (John 2:15–17) and yet was broken inside as he saw the coming destruction of Jerusalem (Luke 19:41-44). Jesus showed a great range of emotion, and yet he was never ruled by those emotions. He was emotionally resilient because he was grounded in God's call upon His life.

In this chapter, we will explore three key areas that ground pastors and help them grow in emotional resilience:

• Processing Criticism and Conflict

• Managing Discouragement and Fatigue

• Cultivating Joy and Gratitude

PROCESSING CRITICISM AND CONFLICT

if possible, so far as it depends on you, being at peace with all men,
Rom 12:18

Criticism is inevitable in ministry. If you have been a pastor any length of time you know this to be true. Even Paul faced relentless criticism from within and outside the church (2 Cor 10–12), yet he remained steadfast, finding his worth in God rather than human opinions of his character, call or ministry.

You must learn how to deal with criticism whether it is warranted and constructive or it is based in falsehood and accusations. Being a pastor will invite scrutiny; therefore, you need skills in navigating those very conflicts. How you handle both types of criticism (constructive or destructive) determines whether they become a source of growth in your life or a gateway to bitterness and relational damage.

As a young pastor I found criticism very difficult to process. Though most of the criticism came from loving friends and church members and was mostly constructive, because of my fragile self-image I recieved it all as hurtful and damaging. Of course, I understood in my head that how I was processing it was completely in error. I could not shake the feelings the words caused in my soul. The result was that I tended to stay away from people if I could. Visitation with members of my church became few and far between and soon the feelings of hurt morphed into feelings of lonliness and relational distance. Though I made some progress through the years, I wasnt until I understood the development of my Dark Side that gave rise to my poor self image, That real strides were made. Take it from me, Learn to process criticism well or it will become a open wound that festers.

Unprocessed criticism often festers into resentment or increased self-doubt. Though my self-image has been very weak over the years. If I didn't learn to process the criticism that I've faced over the years, I don't think I would have lasted these 40 plus years in ministry. Early on I internalized every complaint. I felt each one in my soul and wondered if it was worth it. Pastors often harden themselves and stop listening altogether to protect themselves from the pain and feelings of betrayal.

Healthy processing of criticism involves discernment. Remember, not all criticism is destructive—some is refining. Proverbs teaches us,

RESTORED TO LEAD

Faithful are the wounds of a friend, Pro 27:6

Developing a spiritual emotional resilience means having the humility to learn from what is true and corrective and the maturity to release what is false. It means responding thoughtfully and not reacting to the initial shock or hurt. For me, it was a journey to really believe who I am in Christ rather than believing in what my damaged self said about me. Ultimately all criticism is neutral. It is in how we process it that will either crush us or shape us, all depending on where we place our identity.

What do these Scriptures tell us about the necessity of receiving criticism well?

Bright eyes gladden the heart; A good report puts fat on the bones. He whose ear listens to the life-giving reproof Will lodge among the wise. He who neglects discipline despises his soul, But he who listens to reproof acquires a heart of wisdom. The fear of Yahweh is the discipline leading to wisdom, And before glory comes humility. Proverbs 15:30-33

You have heard that it was said, 'You shall love your neighbor and hate your enemy.' But I say to you, love your enemies and pray for those who persecute you, so that you may be sons of your Father who is in heaven. Matthew 5:43-45a

He has said to me, "My grace is sufficient for you, for power is perfected in weakness." Most gladly, therefore, I will rather boast in my weaknesses, so that the power of Christ may dwell in me. Therefore I am well content with weaknesses, with insults, with distresses, with persecutions and hardships, for the sake of Christ, for when I am weak, then I am strong. 2 Corinthians 12:9–10

Iron sharpens iron, So one man sharpens another. Pro 27:17

...let us consider how to stimulate one another to love and good deeds, Hebrews 10:24

As leaders, you and I must cultivate a heart soft enough to receive correction yet strong enough to stand under criticism without losing peace and spiraling into hurt and bitterness.

MANAGING DISCOURAGEMENT AND FATIGUE

Let us not lose heart in doing good, for in due time we will reap if we do not grow weary. Galatians 6:9

Discouragement is one of the most common experiences in a pastor's life. It can come in a moment's notice – the attendance is down a bit on Sunday, conflict arises, personal struggles don't seem to be going away, spiritual fruit seems scarce or just beyond reach. What can put a pastor over the edge is that other churches grow without even trying or worse, they grow with a leader who is morally compromised. Is there something wrong with me? Does God even care? We spend hours preparing messages, struggle in prayer, pack our counseling schedules full but there seems to be little fruit from all our labors. Over time, this constant and unrelieved discouragement can lead to emotional fatigue, cynicism, or even pastoral burnout.

The prophet Elijah knew these feelings well. After a great victory on Mount Carmel, he fled falling into depression saying, "I have had enough, Lord" (1 Kings 19:4). Even the Apostle Paul reported that at times he was on the verge of collapse

...we were burdened excessively, beyond our strength, so that we despaired even to live. 2 Cor 1:8

Yet in these moments of emotional collapse, God meets them not with rebuke or a sharp "Pull yourself together man!" but with rest, food, the prayers of others, and gentle restoration.

When extended seasons of discouragement arrive, pastors often try to push through rather than pausing for renewal and refocusing (more on this when we talk about the necessity of a firm calling in the next chapter). The only way through these seasons is by building rhythms of rest, reflection, and surrender.

Christopher Ash provides a prayer in his short book that has been helpful to me when I struggle in this area. I would encourage you to write it down or post it someplace prominent, so you have it at hand when discouragement overwhelms.

Lord, make my life of service worth something; make it sure. May it be that, at the end of time, this collection of dust, this temporary mortal frail feeble sinful Christian may have achieved something by your grace that will last to eternity.

Remember fruit is not something we create. It is given by God who brings the growth. So plant and water but release responsibility for growth. Instead, be faithful today and rest in him.

Take 15 minutes and meditate on this Scripture from Psalm 42.

These things I remember as I pour out my soul: how I used to go to the house of God under the protection of the Mighty One with shouts of joy and praise among the festive throng. Why, my soul, are you downcast? Why so disturbed within me? Put your hope in God, for I will yet praise him, my Savior and my God. Psalm 42:5 (NIV)

CULTIVATING JOY AND GRATITUDE

Rejoice in the Lord always; again I will say, rejoice! Phil 4:4

We have an epidemic of grumpy Christians. These brothers and sisters are in every church with frowns on. Sometimes the frowns are on the inside with a fake smile to cover their real self. Yet, you can notice them because they complain about everything and even when they get their way they complain all the more. They may be happy now and then but if things don't go their way true biblical joy is rarely present. If you want to find one, many times they are standing right behind the pulpit.

Biblical joy is not and should not be a fleeting emotion. It is more than the release of chemicals in our brains in reaction to some sort of stimuli. —it is a spiritual discipline and a mark of maturity. James tells us to:

Consider it all joy, my brothers, when you encounter various trials. James 1:2

James' ultimate point is that we can respond to anything that life throws at us with joy because we know God is in control. Whether circumstances in our lives bring heartache and suffering or great contentment and peace, we can respond with joy because we know he is sovereign. We can only experience joy if our faith is in him. Joy comes through faith. So, we choose to trust that God will fulfill every promise he has made and that will produce true joy.

Joy is the fruit of a heart anchored in trust and gratitude

The apostle Paul wrote the words of Philippians 4:4 while imprisoned, proving that joy is possible even in tough times when rooted in Christ rather than circumstances. Gratitude for what God has already done and joy in trusting that he will keep all his promises guard our hearts from bitterness and help sustain emotional balance. When we as pastors consistently focus on what is lacking, ministry becomes the daily grind we just force ourselves to show up for.

Cultivating joy involves practicing praise, celebrating small victories, laughing with loved ones, and remembering that ministry is a privilege, not a punishment. Here's the point: A joyful and grateful pastor will communicate the goodness of God more effectively than any well-crafted sermon can.

Ask yourself these questions as you search your heart. If you want to go a step further take these questions and answer them on a regular basis as you journal and pray.

When was the last time you intentionally praised someone in your congregation? How can you make that a regular practice?

What is one small victory in the past month that you can praise God for?

When was the last time you really laughed? What was the situation that caused that joyful outburst? Is there a rhythm that you can tap into to bring more of these times rather than complaint sessions?

When was the last time you thanked God for calling you into ministry? Are you thankful? If not, what needs to happen practically in your life to regain your gratitude and joy?

Go, eat of the fat, drink of the sweet, and
send portions to him who has nothing
prepared; for this day is holy to our Lord.
Do not be grieved,
for the joy of Yahweh is your strength.
Nehemiah 8:10

Philly G Andrade

PRINCIPLES

1 **Processing Criticism:** Discern truth, release falsehood, stay anchored in God's approval.

2 **Managing Discouragement:** Rest and reflection are essential for resilience.

3 **Cultivating Joy:** Gratitude guards the heart and restores perspective.

REFLECTION

PROCESSING CRITICISM

How do you currently respond to criticism—defensively, despairingly, or with discernment?

What practical steps can you take to separate helpful feedback from harmful attacks?

MANAGING DISCOURAGEMENT

What signs of fatigue do you notice in yourself when your emotional reserves are low?

Who can you talk to honestly about your discouragement?

CULTIVATING JOY

What daily practices help you maintain a grateful heart?

How can you intentionally celebrate God's work, both big and small, in your ministry?

INTEGRATION

Which of these three areas—criticism, discouragement, or joy—requires the most intentional work in your current season?

What will you commit to doing this week to nurture emotional resilience?

THE MAIN POINT

EMOTIONALLY RESILIENT LEADERS FEEL DEEPLY, BUT THEY DO NOT FALL

EASILY BECAUSE THEY ARE ANCHORED IN THE FACT THAT GOD WILL KEEP

ALL HIS PROMISES. AS THE LEADERSHIP GOES SO DOES THE CHURCH.

Phillip G Andrade
PHOTOGRAPHY

"Let us not lose heart in doing good, for in due time we will reap if we do not grow weary.

Galatians 6:9

06

THE FOUNDATION OF A TRUE CALLING

One of the most critical questions every pastor or church leader must ask is this: Am I truly called by God to this work? Despite the good work most seminaries do in training a pastor few ever ask the question: Should you be a pastor? I know of many seminary graduates that finish with advanced degrees and never asked themselves that question. You can be the most talented orator, you can be an expert in biblical languages, you can be a skilled counselor but if you do not have a call then you are bankrupt. The call to fulltime service comes from something more than the skillset.

The call of God is not merely an internal desire or an external recognition from others; it is a divine summons to serve Christ and His Church. Without this genuine calling, ministry can become an unbearable weight rather than a sacred privilege. Without a clear call, there is no unshakeable foundation to go to when the storms come. And they will come.

The apostle Paul opens many of his letters by identifying himself as "called to be an apostle of Christ Jesus by the will of God" (1 Corinthians 1:1). His assurance of divine calling was the anchor that held him steady amid persecution, loneliness, and hardship. Similarly, a true pastoral calling provides stability in seasons of discouragement and uncertainty. It is the deep inner conviction that, no matter how difficult ministry becomes:

"He who calls you is faithful, and He will do it"1 Thess 5:24 (NIV)

Recent research has shown a trend over the years resulting in shorter tenures in churches. A 2011 study revealed a 3.6 year average.[1] Another poll focusing on smaller or plateaued churches showed a 5 year average tenure.[2] This is troubling in that the greatest impact of a pastoral ministry has been shown to occur in years 5-14.

[1] Lifeway Research. "Pastors Feel Privileged and Positive, Though Discouragement Can Come." Lifeway Research. October 5, 2011. Accessed December 28, 2025. https://research.lifeway.com/2011/10/05/pastors-feel-privileged-and-positive-though-discouragement-can-come/.
[2] Barna Group. The State of the Church 2020. Barna Research. Accessed December 28, 2025. https://www.barna.com/collections/the-state-of-the-church-2020/.

When it comes to long term ministry over a lifetime, Ellison Research indicated an average of 19 years total with 15.6 years as average for senior pastorates.[3] Other national samples show similar statistics. Thom Rainer's research in 2016[4] did show 20-40 years for long tenures but also found that the average career ends prematurely, meaning the 40 year range was rare.

As we have discussed in this volume there can be a multiplicity of reasons why a pastor may call it quits. I believe that one of the lesser known causes may be that many of these men have either not been called to ministry or more likely, that the primacy of their call has been forgotten in the "heat of battle."

THE CALL AS THE SOURCE OF ENDURANCE

The ministry is a lifelong marathon, not a sprint, shimmy or cruise. Pastors and leaders who lack a clear sense of calling often find themselves overwhelmed by the relentless pressures of leadership we've talked about—criticism, exhaustion, loneliness, and spiritual attack.

Being overwhelmed is not always because of the extremes such as a moral failure or a lack of key skills—it is often a lack of sustaining conviction that God Himself has placed them there. When we are unsure of our calling, difficulties seem final. When we are certain of it, difficulties become opportunities for growth and faith. Paul's own perseverance was rooted in his confidence of divine appointment:

I am grateful to Christ Jesus our Lord, who has strengthened me, because He regarded me faithful, putting me into service, 1 Tim 1:12

Paul's endurance flowed from his awareness that his role was a sacred trust from God, not a human career choice. It was a privilege that God trusted Paul with. It was a call to partnership where if Paul was faithful God would provide the power for endurance under any circumstance. That confidence, that hope, will provide the bulwark against anything that may come against you from inside or out.

[3] Baptist Press. "Survey: Pastors Say Pastors Should Stop Moving Church to Church." Baptist Press. Accessed December 28, 2025. https://www.baptistpress.com/resource-library/news/survey-pastors-say-pastors-should-stop-moving-church-to-church/#:~:text=Conducted%20by%20Ellison%20Research%20of,pastors%20stay%20in%20one%20position.
[4] Lifeway Research. "10 Traits of Pastors Who Have Healthy Long-Term Tenure." Lifeway Research. September 22, 2016. Accessed December 28, 2025. https://research.lifeway.com/2016/09/22/10-traits-of-pastors-who-have-healthy-long-term-tenure/.

THE DANGER OF A MISPLACED MOTIVATION

Some enter ministry out of good intentions, family tradition, or the desire to help others. While these motives aren't sinful and appear noble, they are insufficient to sustain a pastor through the weight of spiritual warfare and emotional strain that is all too common in ministry. Ministry done in human strength will always lead to burnout and possibly the abuse of God's people. Human abilities and skill sets, a litany of good works and giftedness are not the same as a divine call.

Sometimes men enter ministry without even knowing their real motivations. Often, because of the dark side we previously discussed, some may enter ministry for good intentions while unaware of their inner drive to seek attention. As an introvert myself, I can see how I have sometimes fallen into that trap. Though I am a solid introvert that doesn't release me from the need for approval of others. Though I am sure of my call to ministry, I confess that I sometimes crave the accolades of men and maybe, in a co-dependent sort of way, compromise what is the right thing to do to gain the hearty slap on the back approval. Woe to the one who has no sure calling and enters ministry with misplaced motivation. If you don't have a certain clear call from God, you may find yourself seeking approval from others as your foundation rather than the Call. We can deceive ourselves so much with this that while on the outside people see 'service to God,' on the inside it is truly 'service to self.'

The call of God is not primarily about doing, but about being—being His servant, His shepherd, and His representative. It is birthed in relationship and sustained by obedience not by using the position to prop up self. You cannot be a servant leader if the goal is self.

...doing nothing from selfish ambition or vain glory, but with humility of mind regarding one another as more important than yourselves, not merely looking out for your own personal interests, but also for the interests of others. Phil 2:3-4

DISCERNING THE CALL OF GOD

The call of God can take different forms. For some, it is a getting thrown off a horse clarity, as in Paul's Damascus Road encounter (Acts 9). For others, it is a gradual recognition through the affirmations of mentors, the fruit of ministry, and the inner witness of the Holy Spirit.

Discerning the call involves both the inward witness — *"the Spirit Himself testifies with our spirit,"* (Romans 8:16) and outward confirmation — *"Set apart for Me Barnabas and Saul for the work to which I have called them,"* (Acts 13:2). Healthy discernment also comes through the counsel of wise and mature believers who can confirm the authenticity of one's calling. This is all to say that if you didn't get the 'thrown off a horse' experience then you need to search your inner motives, seek God's Spirit for wisdom, seek the counsel of others (Make sure they are not 'yes men"), assess your giftedness and spiritual maturity level. It may take some work but the work of discerning the Call of God may be the difference between a ministry of years or decades

REFLECTION

Take time to prayerfully reflect on these questions. Use them in solitude, or discuss them with a mentor or trusted peer in ministry.

Can you clearly articulate how God called you into ministry? If not ask: Am I really called to ministry?

When challenges arise, do I rely on my skills or on the assurance that God Himself has placed me here? How has your sense of calling sustained you through those challenges?

ARE YOU CALLED?

Have I ever mistaken a personal desire or expectation from others for a divine call?

Does my calling produce joy and peace even in hardship, or does it feel primarily like obligation and pressure?

How do others—elders, mentors, or my congregation—affirm the evidence of God's call in my life?

In what ways am I nurturing the call of God daily through prayer, study, and obedience?

If God were to call me out of this ministry tomorrow, would I still be content in simply being His servant?

TWO TYPES OF "CALLING"

Sam Rima's book Leading from the Inside Out explains two types of calling that people often mix up.[5]

This confusion, if not cleared up may lead many people into the ministry with a false sense of call. Conversely, a strong sense of call can be the foundation that supports a pastor in tough and uncertain times.

CALLING (CAPITAL C)

YOUR TRUE PURPOSE

In Galatians, Paul explains how God changed him. He went from being a Pharisee who attacked the church to becoming an apostle of that same church. He uses the word καλεω to describe this total change.

> But when God, who had set me apart from my mother's womb and called me through His grace, was pleased to reveal His Son in me so that I might proclaim Him as good news among the Gentiles,...Gal 1:15-16a

Later, Paul writes to the Ephesians. They were struggling with their culture, just like we do today. He reminds them of their call and tells them to "lead a life worthy of your calling" (Ephesians 4:1).

This isn't just for some people. It's not reserved for pastors or missionaries. Everyone who follows Christ shares the same Calling.

> There is one body and one Spirit, just as also you were called in one hope of your calling;Eph 4:4

For Paul, there was only one Calling for Christians. If you follow Jesus, you have one Calling in this life. We're all called to become like Christ. We're waiting for the same future. We're citizens of God's Kingdom, not Babylon. We're heirs with Christ.

[5] Rima, Samuel D. Leading from the Inside Out. Grand Rapids: Baker Books, 2000. 55.

This wasn't just Paul's idea. Peter writes the same thing in his first letter:

But you are a chosen family, a royal priesthood, a holy nation, a people for God's own possession, so that you may proclaim the excellencies of Him who has called you out of darkness into His marvelous light; 1 Peter 2:9

Scripture repeats this truth over and over. Our Calling matters more than any job or career, no matter how much status our culture gives it. Our true purpose as Christians is to be God's special people. We share him with others. We teach them so they can join the called ones too.

This Call answers life's biggest question: What is the meaning of life? When we know our true purpose, our daily work gains deeper meaning. It makes sense in a bigger story. God's Call gives our lives eternal purpose, no matter who we are or what we do for a living.

cALLING (LOWERCASE C)

YOUR JOB

Your calling is your job. It's what you do for work or money. It's how you pay the bills.

Webster calls this a "side job pursued along with your main purpose." Your calling should always come second to your Calling. The work you do can't become the main thing. Your true purpose—the big C Calling—is why you were set apart, why you were born, why you trusted Jesus.

When we connect with our true Calling, we can do real ministry anywhere. It doesn't matter what job we have. We can live out our purpose whether we're in an office, a factory, or a classroom.

This was Paul's secret. Making tents didn't bother him. He didn't see it as a setback. Sitting in prison didn't change anything either. His job or location didn't change his Calling. He knew what his life Calling was, and he knew it was specific to him.

He explains part of it when defending himself in Jerusalem:

And I said, 'What should I do, Lord?' And the Lord said to me, 'Rise up and go on into Damascus, and there you will be told of all that has been determined for you to do.' Acts 22:10

We get more details from what God told Ananias about Paul:

But the Lord said to him, "Go, for he is a chosen instrument of Mine, to bear My name before the Gentiles and kings and the sons of Israel; for I will show him how much he must suffer for My name." Acts 9:15-16

Paul's Calling stayed the same whether he was making tents, preaching in cities, or writing from prison. His job changed, but his purpose didn't.

EXERCISE: YOUR SPECIFIC LIFE CALLING

To the best of your ability, write down what you believe your SPECIFIC calling may be.

Bad examples would be "I am called to be a plumber, fireman or pastor." Those examples give a person's 'lower case calling." Ask; What is my Specific call rooted in my position as a child of God that transcends any job I may hold? For example: "My life's Calling is to partner with God in the transformation of lives through the teaching of God's Word" or "My life's Calling is to serve the disenfranchised people in my community by provided for their basic needs." Both those Callings can be pursued no matter my income source or locality.

I believe the following is my life calling

CONCLUSION

The Call of God is the cornerstone of faithful and long-term ministry. The Call of God is what takes ordinary people of no human fame or report and empowers them to do the work of the kingdom faithfully even if we must suffer for His sake (Acts 9:16). Without a clear Call, ministry becomes work and a heavy burdon that cannot be carried with human strength and effort. With a clear Call, we have something that sustains us when difficult times come. Yes the burden is still there but it becomes light just as Jesus promised.

Your calling is not primarily about what you do, it is focused on Jesus and what he whats to accomplished through you. Though it is MY Calling, it is the work of the one who set you apart and called you.

You did not choose Me but I chose you, and appointed you that you would go and bear fruit, and that your fruit would abide, so that whatever you ask of the Father in My name He may give to you. John 15:16

ARE YOU CALLED?

Walk worthy of the calling with which you have been called,..

Ephesians 4:1

UNHEALTHY LEADERSHIP

07

UNHEALTHY LEADERSHIP

SERVANT LEADERSHIP VS. THE MESSIAH COMPLEX

Pastoral ministry, at its heart, is a divine invitation to serve—to serve God with wholehearted devotion, to serve His church with complete commitment and to serve the advance of the Gospel to every heart. Step back from the busyness of your calling just for a moment. It is a beautiful thing God has entrusted to you -beautiful beyond imagination but at the same time not at all easy because it will eventually call us to sacrifice. The problem is that there are two kinds of sacrifice.

There is a Christ-like sacrifice that leaves you weary in the moment yet powerfully renewed in the long run—because it flows from obedience to the Gospel and love for God. There is a self-focused sacrifice that looks spiritual on the outside while on the inside you are being withered away. In my 40+ years of ministry I has dipped my toes in the latter all too often and it did not work out well for me or for the people in my care. Jesus sets the standard for healthy leadership.

> *For even the Son of Man did not come to be served, but to serve, and to give His life a ransom for many." Mark 10:45*

Not only does Jesus tell us the nature of his leadership in the passage above, he goes on to demonstrate it to those who would become leaders after he ascends.

> *So when He had washed their feet, and taken His garments and reclined at the table again, He said to them, "Do you know what I have done to you? You call Me Teacher and Lord; and you are right, for so I am. If I then, the Lord and the Teacher, washed your feet, you also ought to wash one another's feet. For I gave you an example that you also should do as I did to you. John 13:12-15*

The aim of this chapter is to help you discern the difference and to fix your ministry firmly in servant leadership rather than in the subtle, seductive pull of a messiah complex. The goal is to be a shepherd not a savior.

THE NATURE OF HEALTHY SACRIFICE

Healthy sacrifice is always patterned after Jesus, the Good Shepherd who laid down His life for the sheep (John 10:11). Jesus was purposeful, Spirit-directed, and rooted in love rather than compulsion. Paul summarizes the attitude of Christ in this well known passage.

Do nothing from selfish ambition or conceit, but in humility count others more significant than yourselves. Let each of you look not only to his own interests, but also to the interests of others. Have this mind among yourselves, which is yours in Christ Jesus, who, though he was in the form of God, did not count equality with God a thing to be grasped, but emptied himself, by taking the form of a servant, being born in the likeness of men,..Philippians 2:3-8 (ESV)

Healthy sacrifice is marked by five clear characteristics:

- **It Aligns With Genuine Calling** The sacrifices we offer should flow directly from the Calling we talked about in the previous chapter As elders/pastors we carry out the specifics of our Call by teaching the Word, equipping the saints, guarding healthy doctrine, and loving the church. Anything consistently outside the contours of our Calling and giftedness deserves careful scrutiny.(1 Pet 5:2–4; Eph 4:11–13, Titus 1).

- **It Is Discerned, Not Assumed** Jesus repeatedly withdrew from crowds to pray (Luke 5:16) and deliberately chose which villages to enter and which sick to heal on any given day. Discernment—through Scripture, prayer, and wise counsel—is the antidote to the reflexive "yes" that so often plagues pastors. As Eugene Peterson reminded us, "The adjective busy set as a modifier to pastor should sound to our ears like adulterous to characterize a wife[1]"

- **It Honors God-Given Human Limitations** We are not infinite. Jesus slept in storms (Mark 4:38), ate when hungry, and delegated ministry to imperfect disciples. Healthy sacrifice acknowledges that we are finite creatures. We are not bugged, it is how we were designed. The Sabbath is not a suggestion; it is a theological declaration that God, not us, keeps the world spinning.

- **It Produces Life, Not Just Activity** Kingdom sacrifice may exhaust us temporarily, but it should ultimately bear fruit that remains (John 15:16). If our pattern of sacrifice consistently leaves us depleted, cynical, bitter or relationally distant, something is misaligned.

[1] Peterson, Eugene. The Contemplative Pastor: Returning to the Art of Spiritual Direction. Eerdmans. 1989. 21

• **It Is Shared, Not Solo** Healthy sacrifice multiplies itself by inviting the entire body to participate (Eph 4:12, 16). The pastor is never the sole bearer of ministry; we are called to equip others to bear it with us.

THE NATURE OF UNHEALTHY SACRIFICE

Unhealthy sacrifice is a master of disguise. It begins quietly, disguised as devotion. It whispers, "If you don't do it, no one will," or "Good pastors are always available." Over time, these whispers calcify into patterns that erode both leader and church.

Unhealthy sacrifice reveals itself in four recurring markers:

• **It Attempts to Meet Every Need** – creating a culture of pastoral dependency rather than disciple maturity. This was a hard lesson for me to learn. You don't have to do things that others leave undone. You don't have to pick up every football that someone drops on the field. I often would justify this unhealthy pattern by saying to myself that "God deserves our excellence in all things, so I will fill all the gaps for excellence sake." While it is true that God deserves our excellence it is untrue that I have to be the only one striving for it. We need to train and encourge people to pick up the ball and sometimes, if they don't, leave it on the field.

• **It Consistently Neglects Personal and Family Health** – treating spouse, children, sleep, and emotional margin as optional luxuries. Your first ministry to to your family. If you do not guard this like a warrior the pressures of ministry will damage them.

• **It Arises from Compulsion, Not Conviction** – driven by guilt, fear of criticism, or an unexamined need to be needed. If you have a shred of co-dependency in you, there will be a temptaion to compromise the right thing to get pats on the back. Lead from conviction and principle or you will find yourself running around doing everything with no purpose but to please others. Focus on pleasing Jesus alone. All my children have been raised with this saying:"Live for an audience of One." Model it and you may find your children and people living it out.

• **It Ignores or Despises Limits** – viewing rest as unfaithful and boundaries as selfish. More on this next chapter.

I remember a seasons in my ministry when I believed the fate of the entire church rested on my shoulders. I preached and taught Sunday School every Sunday, Conducted 2 or 3 small groups throughout the week, counseled people when I should have been home with my family, I answered the phones, ran the youth group and did the bulletin. My calling became the thing that "stole Daddy away." The breaking point came when I found myself angry at the very people I was supposedly "laying down my life" for. It was a wake-up call that I had adopted the identity of savior. Any problem? No problem, Pastor Phil will fix it.

THE PASTORAL IDENTITY AND THE MESSIAH COMPLEX

The dividing line between healthy and unhealthy sacrifice is almost always identity. When our sense of self is securely rooted in our relationship with Jesus (Gal 2:20; Col 3:3), we serve from a place of humility and dependence. When our identity becomes fused with performance, perception, or indispensability, we drift—often unconsciously—into a messiah complex.

Clinical psychologist Diane Langberg, who has worked with countless burned-out Christian leaders, describes this dynamic with painful clarity:

"We begin to believe that we are the ones holding it all together...We become functional atheists, living as though everything depends on us[2]*"*

[2] Langberg, Diane. Suffering and the Heart of God: How Trauma Destroys and Christ Restores. New Growth Press, 2015. 87.

REFLECTION

There are seven common symptoms that may indicate a messiah complex taking root in your life.

Rank the following 7 questions prayerfully from one indicating "Never" to ten indicating "All the Time"

Do I have an inability to separate personal identity from pastoral role?

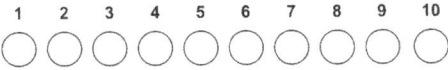

Do you have a subtle belief that the church cannot survive without your direct involvement?

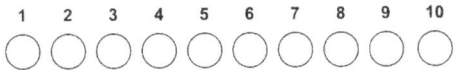

Do you feel you carry ultimate responsibility for other people's spiritual growth?

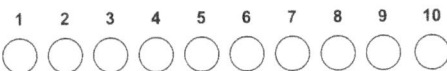

Are you unable to rest without guilt or anxiety?

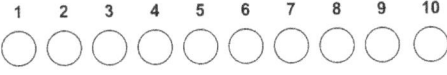

Are you functioning as the primary (or only) caregiver rather than equipper in your church?

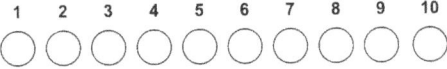

Do you feel threatened when others step into leadership?

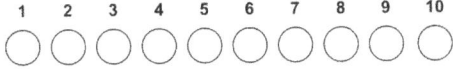

UNHEALTHY LEADERSHIP

Do you feel shame or get defensive when someone suggests you need help?

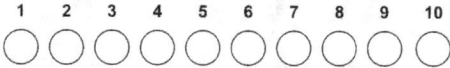

Look at the numbers above. Any high numbers in more than two or three of the questions may indicate a real problem with your identity and potential to burnout. Of course, any honest pastor will see at least traces of these tendencies in their own heart. The issue is not whether we are tempted; the issue is whether we name and renounce the temptation as not what the Lord desires from us.

SERVANT LEADERSHIP AS THE BIBLICAL ANTIDOTE

Servant leadership dismantles the messiah complex by relentlessly returning ultimate responsibility to Christ and meaningful responsibility to the body.

Oswald Sanders in his classic *Spiritual Leadership* describes servant leadership as authority exercised through service, humility, and character. That is, a leader's power is expressed as influence for others' spiritual growth rather than self-exaltation.[3]

The quintessential book on Christian leadership is Clinton's *The Making of a Leader*. Clinton writes a concise definition of the nature of Christian leadership.

"Leadership is a dynamic process in which a man or woman with God-given capacity influences a specific group of God's people toward His purposes for the group.[4]"

Both these definitions or frameworks give us a basic understanding of how to practically lead day after day. Biblical Leadership isn't about office, title, or human measures — but about a God-given calling and responsibility to guide God's people toward God's purposes. We lead not like the authorites in the world do, rather leadership is expressed through service of others, not self. Leadership is based in character not position or the word 'Reverend' before your name. This is Jesus point in Matthew 20:

You know that the rulers of the Gentiles lord it over them, and their great men exercise authority over them. It is not this way among you, but whoever wishes to become great among you shall be your servant, and whoever wishes to be first among you shall be your slave;
Mt 20:25b-27

True servant leaders:

• See themselves as stewards, not saviors.

• Empower rather than enable.

• Practice life-giving rhythms of work and rest.

[3] Sanders, Oswald. Spiritual Leadership. 1st ed. Chicago: Moody Publishers, 2017.
[4] Clinton, J. Robert. The Making of a Leader: Recognizing the Lessons and Stages of Leadership Development. Colorado Springs: NavPress, 1988.

• Serve from overflow rather than from a perpetually empty tank.

• Cultivate churches where every member is both cared for and caring, served and serving.

If you are a church leaders you has been given a great privilege in being entrusted with the things of God. We are now called to take that privilege and be faithful with it.

Let a man consider us in this manner, as servants of Christ and stewards of the mysteries of God. In this case, moreover, it is required of stewards that one be found faithful. 1 Cor 4:1–2

WHAT IS YOUR REAL MOTIVATION?

Do I rush to fulfill needs out of genuine love or out of fear of what will happen if I don't? What is my real motivation?

Does this sacrifice flow from obedience to Christ or from an unexamined need to be the hero?

Am I empowering others to walk in their gifts, or am I keeping ministry safe by keeping it manageable (and centered on me)?

1 Peter 2:5 clearly teaches the priesthood of all believers. Do you live and serve as though you really believe it?

A FINAL WORD

Ministry is not a sprint of heroic effort; it is a lifetime of faithful presence. Christ never asked us to carry what only He can bear. He asked us to abide in Him, to love as we have been loved, and to shepherd His sheep with the same gentle strength He shows us.

May we have the courage to lay down our lives—and the wisdom to know when picking them back up again is the most Christlike thing we can do.

REFLECTION

When you think about your ministry sacrifices, which feel healthy and life-giving? Which feel heavy, obligatory, or unhealthy?

Have you ever felt that the church could not function without you? How did that belief shape your behavior?

In what ways do you see elements of a messiah complex influencing your ministry decisions?

How do you discern between God-led sacrifice and guilt-driven overcommitment?

What story from your ministry journey best illustrates the difference between healthy and unhealthy sacrifice?

What is one God-honoring boundary you can implement this week to guard your pastoral identity?

LIMITS

08

BOUNDARIES, PERSONAL SCHEDULES, AND THE ART OF SAYING "NO."

The pastorate is one of the few jobs I know where people praise you when you work yourself to death and quietly judge you when you refuse to.

Have you ever experienced something similar to this? The day begins with a call that a church member has died and the family needs immediate care. You try to make time but there is also a couple in your church thats on the verge of divorce and they want to meet tonight. It happens to be Friday and your sermon is half finished because you have been struggling with "sermon block" and find it hard to put words down on paper. Someone just posted a question on the church Facebook page asking why the pastor doesn't respond in a timely fashion to questions posted there. The youth pastor calls in at the last minute and says that he can't be there tonight because of a family emergency. He says you can cancel but the youth have already started arriving for the meeting. Your wife calls and asks that you come home right away because the dog ate something that is causing him to vomit all over the house.

Have you ever been there? The needs never end and there is always a fire to put out. The expectation—spoken or unspoken—is that the pastor will meet all those needs and expectations. All of them. All of the time.

I have lived in that tension for much of my ministry. I have also learned, usually the hard way, that healthy boundaries are not the enemy of faithful ministry. Without boundaries serving God can be transformed into something God never intended. The love for the people will slowly turn into resentment of them. Rather than serving from the heart it simply becomes compulsion and if the pattern continues, the pastor often become the first casualty.

This chapter is an invitation to steward your life in such a way that you can love God, love your family, and love your church for decades—not just for the next crisis cycle.

THE PURPOSE AND POWER OF BOUNDARIES

Biblical healthy boundaries should not be walls that keep bad things out rather they are that which keep the good things in. They protect the very resources—emotional health, spiritual power, relational depth—that make authentic long-term ministry possible.

Henry Cloud and John Townsend famously defined a boundary as "a property line" that clarifies ownership and responsibility.[1]

In pastoral life, boundaries declare what is mine to carry and what is not, what is mine to give and what must be released to God and to others. We talked about this idea of responsibilities in a previous chapter. Now lets dig a little deeper into this idea of the division of responsibilities.

When we have loose boundaries and confused responsibilities there are a number of issues that can arise:

• Chronic overcommitment and adrenaline addiction (increased risk of heart attack)[2]

• Compassion fatigue and emotional burnout[3]

• Erosion of family relationships and personal identity often resulting in a decrease of marital intimacy and chronic depression.

• Physical fatigue that impacts the ability to excel in the call. This may include the lack of desire to preach and teach, decreased desire to be with your people and eventually a diminished amount of spiritual capital and authority.

In my first senior pastorate, I served without boundaries for almost 20 years. For 20 years I answered every call, attended every meeting, and visited every hospital room, filled every ministry hole, and strived to be the example to follow. I was proud of my availability and sacrifice—until I slowly realized my children were saddened when the phone rang and daddy had to go. I realized my prayer life had become a string of desperate pleas rather than an intimate conversation with the Lord. I became aware that my sermons, though well crafted and biblical, were devoid of the passion I had for the Word. That season taught me two very important principles. First, boundless availability is not the same as boundless love. They may look the

[1] Cloud, Henry, and John Townsend. Boundaries: When to Say Yes, How to Say No to Take Control of Your Life. Grand Rapids: Zondervan, 1992.
[2] Mayo Clinic. "Stress Management: Understand and Manage Stress." Mayo Clinic. Accessed December 28, 2025. https://www.mayoclinic.org/healthy-lifestyle/stress-management/in-depth/stress/art-20046037. Chen, H.-Y., Liu, T.-T., and Hsu, T.-Y. "Effects of Stress on Health and Wellness: A Review of the Literature." PubMed Central (PMC). Accessed December 28, 2025. https://pmc.ncbi.nlm.nih.gov/articles/PMC4084669/.
[3] Figley, Charles R., ed. Compassion Fatigue: Coping with Secondary Traumatic Stress Disorder in Those Who Treat the Traumatized. New York: Brunner/Mazel, 1995.

same to others but inside the motivation and source of power are much different.

Secondly, God's grace finds us even when we flounder and damage ourselves. I am surprised my family and I survived with so few scars. God is sovereign and he certainly will work through our brokeness, messy boundaries and lack of clarity but he would much rather work through a pastor who though weak, has learned to keep healthy boundaries and seek clarity and discernment by any means. Steven Cole commenting on 2 Timothy 2:20-26 writes:

> *"The opportunity to be used or not used is based on our actions. We can all be used by God; however, the extent is up to us... If someone cleanses himself of such behavior, he will be a vessel for honorable use, set apart, useful to the Master, prepared for every good work.[4]"*

THE PASTORAL SCHEDULE AS A THEOLOGICAL DECLARATION

Consider this: How you schedule your life is not neutral. How you spend your days is how you spend your life—and it reveals what you truly believe about God, yourself, and the church. Every pastor will inherit, to some degree, a church DNA shaped by decades of congregational expectation, denominational tradition, and unspoken assumptions. In the same way, the pastor brings his own set of expectations, traditions and assumptions to the congregation. Often these things come into conflict and rather than finding the appropriate boundaries and establishing clear responsibilities and expectations, many pastors will try to fulfill those competing expectations, traditions and assumptions.

So a weekly rhythm often looks like this: Sunday is consumed by services and meeting in the moment needs, Monday is recovery unless something comes up (and it always does), Tuesday through Thursday are a blur of meetings and crises, figuring out how the system of the church is working. Maybe squeeze in some time for personal prayer and learning, Friday is frantic sermon finishing, and Saturday is theoretically a day off but more likely the catch up day. That schedule seems normal for most pastors, but hear me, it is not sustainable, nor healthy for the pastor or the congregation.

A sustainable schedule, by contrast, reflects three non-negotiable categories of time:

---

4 Bible.org. "7. Becoming the Person God Can Greatly Use (2 Timothy 2:20-26)." Bible.org. Accessed December 28, 2025. https://bible.org/seriespage/7-becoming-person-god-can-greatly-use-2-timothy-220-26.

LIMITS

- **Predictable Rhythms** – the recurring tasks that form the backbone of ministry: sermon preparation, worship planning, staff meetings, discipleship appointments, administration. These are planned out times that are nonnegatioable. Do not fall into the trap that everything is a crisis that needs immediate attention. Most things are not. They may seem like they are to the person who calls you but part of your call is to help people think responsibly and take responsibility.

- **Protected Space** – non-negotiable blocks for study, prayer, strategic thinking, self care and family time. Family time is the first thing to be sacrificed on the altar of urgency—and the most costly sacrifice we can make.

- **Responsive Margin** – intentional white space that allows you to weep with those who weep, come along side people in dark times and serve the broken without destroying the rest of the week.

The following questions will help you think through what these catagories might look like in your unique ministry setting.

SCHEDULE ASSESSMENT

Rate each statement on a scale of 1-10 (1 = Strongly Disagree, 10 = Strongly Agree). Calculate the average score for each category to plot on a spider/radar chart with three axes: Predictable Rhythms, Protected Space, and Responsive Margin.

Predictable Rhythms (Questions 1-10)

I consistently schedule and protect time for sermon preparation.

1 2 3 4 5 6 7 8 9 10
◯ ◯ ◯ ◯ ◯ ◯ ◯ ◯ ◯ ◯

Worship planning is blocked out in advance and rarely interrupted.

1 2 3 4 5 6 7 8 9 10
◯ ◯ ◯ ◯ ◯ ◯ ◯ ◯ ◯ ◯

Staff meetings occur at predictable, fixed times.

1 2 3 4 5 6 7 8 9 10
◯ ◯ ◯ ◯ ◯ ◯ ◯ ◯ ◯ ◯

Discipleship appointments are scheduled and honored regularly.

1 2 3 4 5 6 7 8 9 10
◯ ◯ ◯ ◯ ◯ ◯ ◯ ◯ ◯ ◯

Administrative tasks are integrated into my routine without overload.

1 2 3 4 5 6 7 8 9 10
◯ ◯ ◯ ◯ ◯ ◯ ◯ ◯ ◯ ◯

I avoid treating every request as an immediate crisis.

1 2 3 4 5 6 7 8 9 10
◯ ◯ ◯ ◯ ◯ ◯ ◯ ◯ ◯ ◯

I encourage others to take responsibility for non-urgent issues.

1 2 3 4 5 6 7 8 9 10
◯ ◯ ◯ ◯ ◯ ◯ ◯ ◯ ◯ ◯

Recurring tasks form the solid backbone of my ministry.

1 2 3 4 5 6 7 8 9 10
◯ ◯ ◯ ◯ ◯ ◯ ◯ ◯ ◯ ◯

I plan these rhythms ahead to avoid last-minute disruptions.

1 2 3 4 5 6 7 8 9 10
○○○○○○○○○○

I maintain boundaries around predictable tasks during busy seasons.

1 2 3 4 5 6 7 8 9 10
○○○○○○○○○○

Protected Space (Questions 11-20)

I protect dedicated blocks for personal prayer.

1 2 3 4 5 6 7 8 9 10
○○○○○○○○○○

Study time is scheduled and rarely compromised.

1 2 3 4 5 6 7 8 9 10
○○○○○○○○○○

I allocate non-negotiable time for strategic thinking.

1 2 3 4 5 6 7 8 9 10
○○○○○○○○○○

Self-care activities are built into my routine as essentials.

1 2 3 4 5 6 7 8 9 10
○○○○○○○○○○

Family time is prioritized over ministry urgency.

1 2 3 4 5 6 7 8 9 10
○○○○○○○○○○

I enforce boundaries to safeguard personal renewal.

1 2 3 4 5 6 7 8 9 10
○○○○○○○○○○

I spend quality AND quantity time with my wife and family.

1 2 3 4 5 6 7 8 9 10
○○○○○○○○○○

I avoid work intrusions during family or rest periods.

1 2 3 4 5 6 7 8 9 10
○○○○○○○○○○

I recognize the cost of sacrificing protected time and adjust.

1 2 3 4 5 6 7 8 9 10
○○○○○○○○○○

Accountability helps me maintain these non-negotiable blocks.

1 2 3 4 5 6 7 8 9 10
○○○○○○○○○○

Responsive Margin (Questions 21-30)

I build white space into my schedule for unexpected needs.

1 2 3 4 5 6 7 8 9 10
○○○○○○○○○○

I have a sufficient margin that allows me to support those in grief effectively.

1 2 3 4 5 6 7 8 9 10
○○○○○○○○○○

I can respond to crises without derailing my week.

1 2 3 4 5 6 7 8 9 10
○○○○○○○○○○

Flexible time helps me serve others sustainably.

1 2 3 4 5 6 7 8 9 10
○○○○○○○○○○

I set limits to prevent margin from overtaking other areas.

1 2 3 4 5 6 7 8 9 10
○○○○○○○○○○

My schedule includes buffers for spontaneous pastoral care.

1 2 3 4 5 6 7 8 9 10
○○○○○○○○○○

Past lack of margin has shown me its importance.

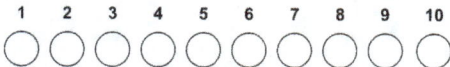

I adjust white space for seasonal ministry demands.

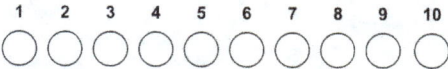

My margin allows for empathy without resentment.

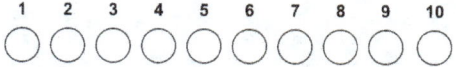

Overall, my margin supports balanced, compassionate ministry.

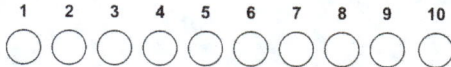

To visualize results: Average each category's scores (out of 10) and plot on the three-axis spider chart below. A balanced profile forms an equilateral shape; imbalances highlight areas for growth.

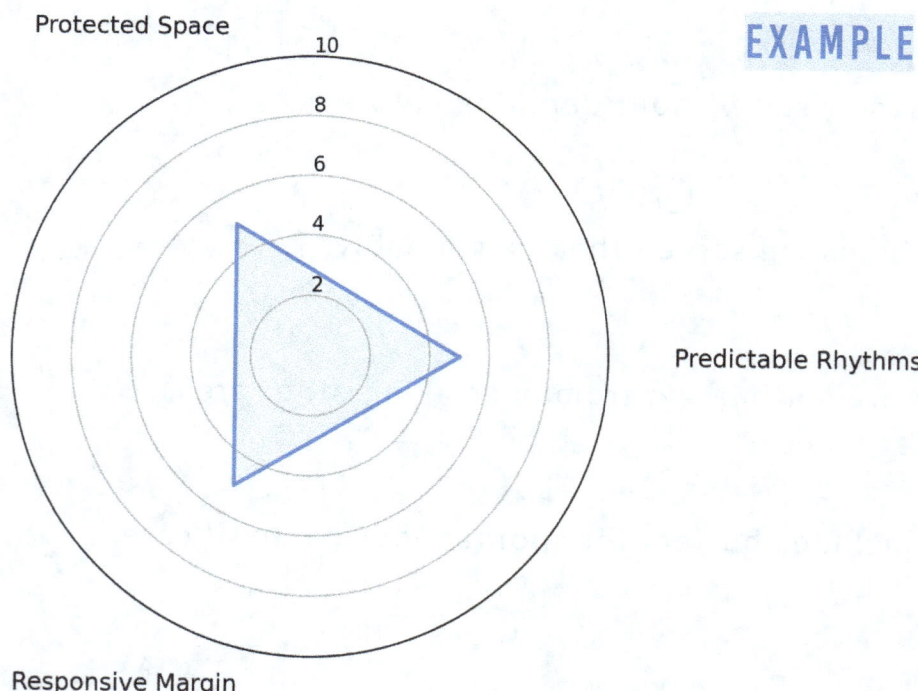

REFLECTION

PREDICTABLE RHYTHMS

What criteria can I use to distinguish between genuine crises and issues that feel urgent but can be handled responsibly by others or at a later time?

In what ways might I communicate boundaries around these predictable rhythms to my congregation or staff to foster their own sense of responsibility?

How do my current habits contribute to or detract from treating these rhythms as the backbone of my ministry, and what adjustments could make them more sustainable?

What systems or tools could I implement to plan these tasks in advance, ensuring they remain non-negotiable even during busier seasons?

PROTECTED SPACE

What specific blocks of time each week or month should I designate as protected for prayer, study, and strategic thinking, and how will I enforce these as non-negotiable?

How has sacrificing family time in the past impacted my well-being and ministry effectiveness, and what steps can I take to prevent this from happening again?

What accountability measures, such as sharing my schedule with a spouse or mentor, could help me maintain these protected spaces amid ministry demands?

How much intentional white space should I build into my weekly schedule to allow for unexpected pastoral care, such as supporting those in grief or crisis?

What boundaries can I set around this responsive margin to ensure it doesn't expand and consume the predictable rhythms or protected spaces?

LIMITS

How might I evaluate and adjust this margin seasonally, based on predictable peaks in ministry needs like holidays or community events?

THE COURAGE TO SAY "NO."

Everytime you say "yes," in someway, you say "no." Every "yes" carries a hidden "no." The question is whether you will choose your nos intentionally or let them be chosen for you by the circumstance.

Five questions will save your minstry. These questions refer back to the three categories of responsibility I introduced in Chapter 4.

1. Is this mine to do? (Does it align with my primary calling in this season?)

2. Is this someone else's opportunity to grow? (Am I robbing another leader of development?)

3. Am I trying to be the Savior in this situation?

4. Do I have the capacity to do this with excellence and joy?

5. What will this cost the people who have the first claim on my life—God, my spouse, my children?

Learning to say no graciously is a spiritual discipline. I don't know where I first heard this from but it is a great script to have running in your head when confronted with these sort of questions. Put it in your own way and make sure it from your heart. It goes something like this:

"I care deeply about this, and because I want to serve you well, I need to say no right now. Here's who can help…"

That response done in a spirit of love and grace will not only protect your soul, it will also empower dozens of emerging leaders that God has sent your way.

THE ART EVERYONE HATES: DELEGATION

Many pastors approach ministry tasks with the philosophy "If I let go, it won't get done right." I understand this fear intimately. There's a certain twisted comfort in believing that only you can visit Mrs. Smith properly, only you can lead that Bible study and not teach some horrific heresy, only you can answer that late-night phone call with adequate pastoral skill and compassion.

The irony is that refusing to delegate these things almost guarantees those things won't get done right long-term, because the pastor will eventually collapse and the people will never be equipped. I've come close to living this way myself though I would have labeled it as "faithfullness." The pastor who insists on being the go to guy in all things, eventually becomes unavailable—through burnout, bitterness, or physical breakdown.

SHARED LEADERSHIP

Biblical leadership is never solo; it is always shared. Moses needed Jethro's wisdom to see that he was "wearing himself out" by trying to judge every dispute alone (Exodus 18:13–27). The apostles recognized that even feeding widows—vital, holy work—required delegation so they could focus on prayer and the Word (Acts 6:1–7). Paul's vision of the church in Ephesians 4:11–16 is a body where every joint supplies, where growth comes from the whole body working together, not from one exhausted shepherd doing everything like some spiritual combination of Superman and the Flash.

Here's a hard truth I've had to accept - When we refuse to delegate, we're not being more faithful, we're being more controlling. This pattern will eventually result in taking from others the joy and spriitual growth that comes through serving.

The Four Pillars of Effective Delegation

So we need to learn to delegate, not only for the sake of others but for our own self-care lest we burnout long before our call is complete. When delegating ministry tasks and plans it will, of course, require us to trust broken people (just like Jesus trusts you) and it will require some practical structure as well.

- BE CLEAR ON THE OUTCOME Don't just assign a task; give them a vision and steps to success. Let them know why you think that they are the perfect match for the job. So don't just say "Can you handle hospital visits," but "Can you visit within 24 hours, pray with the patient, coordinate meal needs with the care team, and report back any critical concerns. I'll support you but you got this!" If you give a vague assingment you will produce vague results, frustrated volunteers and possible increased work for yourself effectively attaining the opposite of what you planned.

- GIVE THEM RESPONSIBILITY WITH AUTHORITY I know this is diificult in some church structures but do all you can within your context to make this happen otherwise it will not be true delegation but simply micro-managemnt. If you ask someone to lead the missions ministry, give them an actual budget and decision-making power. Nothing demoralizes a servant faster than being given responsibility without authority, forced to come back to you for every small decision.

- TRAIN AND COACH THEM Delegation should not be abandonment. The first few hospital visits should be done together. The first few small group discussions should include debriefing. You're not just offloading work; you're equipping God's people (Eph 4:11-12). This is a pastor's primary call in Paul's theology.

- CELEBRATE When that Bible study was lead with skill and knowledge say so—from the pulpit, in the newsletter, in the elders' meeting, shout it from the rooftops. When the event goes well with extraordinary skill and planning, praise the person publically. People tend to rise to the level of recognition they receive. Plus the whole congregation gets the truth that ministry happens through the body, not just through you. My congregation doesn't need me to do everything. They need me to equip everyone. So does yours.

MORE SPACE MEANS MORE LIMITS

Delegation creates space. But space must be filled with something, or it will simply fill with more work. This is where rhythm becomes essential. We disscussed some of these at length already, but it is suffice to say that you have to choose how you fill and how you limit your time and resources. Here are some practical suggestions that are meant to be tailored for your specific situation.

1. Begin every day with Scripture and silence before God End the day the same way

2. Set aside clear times for prayer, sermon preparation and serious study. The phone is in another room. The email is closed. The world will not end if you remove distractions.

3. Exercise and move every day.

4. Commit to device-free dinners with family. This has always been tough and neglected in my life. Don't waste this time. Treat it as sacred because it is.

5. Take time off as your 'sabbath and rest' weekly. 1 day minimum, 2 days preferable because one day can be a true sabbath (No email, no texts, no phone calls, no leadership pressure worrys) and one dayt for fun, family and friends.

6. Protect your study days. Reserve two days for deep preparation. Not administrative work, not counseling appointments, not returning phone calls. Study. Reading. Writing. Thinking. The Sunday sermon deserves this, and so does the congregation.

7. Have one focused pastoral care day. One day for hospital visits, counseling, coffee with struggling members. It's all batched, all intentional, all finished by dinner.

8. Family night and date night' etched into tablets of steel. One night for familiy and kids, one night for my wife. In recent years, because my wife works close to my office, I try to take lunch with her as much as possible. On average I see her for that precious half hour three to four times a week. Our marriage is better for it.

Of course emergencies can interrupt this, but emergencies are rare when expectations are clear.

FACING THE FEAR AND FREEDOM

When I went away for my recent sabbatical I was terrified that the church would fall apart. At the same time I was also afraid that everything would go great without me. See? You're not really needed. They're fine without you.

When I returned, I found that everything was going well. The people had learned somethings, the elders did a fantastic job pastoring and filling the pulpit. They even handled a big crisis while I was gone telling me that I needed to stay on sabbatical. The church had discovered it could survive—even thrive—without me constantly hovering. I realized that too. The church and I also realized together that we, in fact, need each other becuse though they could still be the church without me, they could also be the church with me. That we needed each other. We discovered, in a very vivid way, the truth of Romans 12.

For through the grace given to me I say to each one among you not to think more highly of himself than he ought to think; but to think so as to have sound thinking, as God has allotted to each a measure of faith. For just as we have many members in one body and all the members do not have the same function, so we, who are many, are one body in Christ, and individually members one of another, Rom 12:3-5

That discovery was one of the healthiest things that ever happened to us. Why? A church that can't function without the pastor is a church with a pastor-shaped idol. When that pastor leaves, burns out or falls, the whole thing collapses. A healthy church is a body where every member functions,

168

where the pastor equips but doesn't monopolize, where ministry is shared in the power of His Spirit.

A SPECIAL NOTE ON DIGITAL LIMITS

Smartphones have made pastors more accessible than ever—and more neurotic than ever. My phone's ring tone is the theme from the Good the Bad and The Ugly. I though I was quite the comedian when I added that to my phone. But it's not so funny when the phone goes off during dinner or a text dings during family time saying "I know your busy but I have a question about Proverbs 11:22."

Unless being more neurotic is a life goal, I would suggest putting some boundaries on these electronic tormentors.

- Auto-reply after 7 p.m.: "I'll respond tomorrow during office hours unless this is an emergency. If this is truly urgent, please call the church office and leave a message indicating it's an emergency." This trains people and protects your evening.

- If you can swing the cost, A separate "pastor phone" that stays at the office on days off. Your personal cell is for personal relationships. The church phone stays at church when you're not on duty. If someone needs you urgently, they know how to reach a staffmember or elder

- Social media sabbaticals during sermon preparation. Stay off the social media apps on study days. The outrage, the opinions, the endless scroll—it all poisons the well from which you're trying to draw living water.

Remember, you will have boundaries. The question is whether you'll set them intentionally or let them be set by the loudest voice, the latest crisis, the most insistent personality.

BOUNDARIES AS AN DEMONSTRATION OF FAITH

Healthy boundaries are not selfish. They show by the way we live that these following things are true.

God is sovereign. The church does not depend on your constant vigilance. Jesus holds it together. When you rest, you're confessing that he's enough.

The church belongs to Jesus, not to me. You are a steward, not an owner. A shepherd, not a savior. The church was his before you arrived, and it will be his after you leave. Your boundaries remind everyone—including you—whose church this really is.

My family is my first ministry. If you lose your marriage to save the church, you've lost. If your children grow up resenting ministry because it stole their father, you've failed. The best gift you can give the church is a healthy, joy-filled family that makes the gospel attractive.

My soul is worth protecting. You cannot give what you do not have. A depleted, anxious, resentful pastor does not serve the church well, no matter how many hours he works. Protecting your soul—through rest, boundaries, prayer, friendship—is not selfishness. It's stewardship.

The longest-serving, most fruitful pastors I know are not the ones who burned brightest for a decade. They are the ones who learned to burn steadily for fifty years. They said no when no was wise. They rested when rest was needed. They delegated when delegation was right. They protected their marriages, their schedules, their souls.

REFLECTION QUESTIONS

When have you experienced the negative effects of poor boundaries in ministry?

Which aspects of your weekly schedule consistently create stress or exhaustion?

What responsibilities do you currently carry that someone else could carry with training?

When do you feel guilty when saying "no"? Why?

How would your life and ministry change if you consistently protected time for study, prayer, and rest?

What expectations (spoken or unspoken) from your congregation need clarification or adjustment?

What internal beliefs or assumptions keep you from setting stronger boundaries?

What is one boundary you can implement this week that would immediately improve your well-being?

PASTORAL LIMITS SELF-ASSESSMENT

Rate each statement on a scale from 1 to 10, where:
1 = Strongly disagree / Not true of me
10 = Strongly agree / Very true of me

A. Boundaries and Availability

I maintain clear boundaries around my availability.

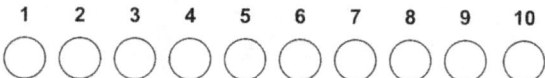

I can say "no" without excessive guilt or fear.

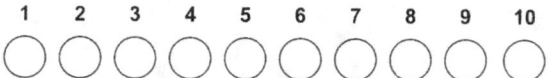

My congregation understands my limits and respects them.

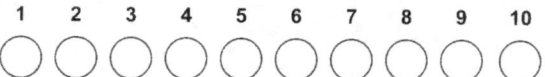

I do not feel pressured to respond immediately to every message or request.

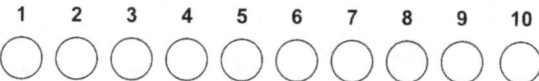

I have established guidelines for digital communication (email, texts, social media).

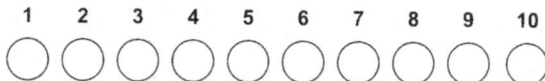

B. Time Management and Schedule

I regularly protect uninterrupted time for sermon preparation.

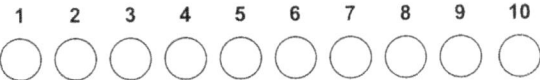

I have structured times for pastoral care, administration, and planning.

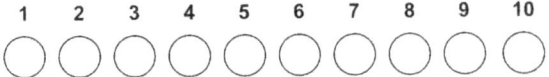

My schedule includes margin for unplanned needs.

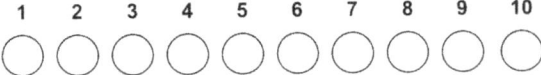

I review and adjust my weekly rhythms intentionally.

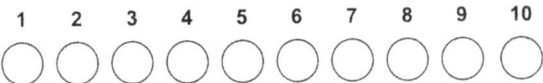

I regularly prioritize tasks based on calling, impact, and capacity.

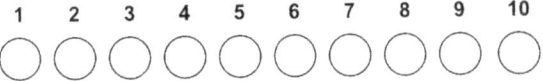

C. Sustainable Rhythms

I keep a weekly Sabbath that is truly restorative.

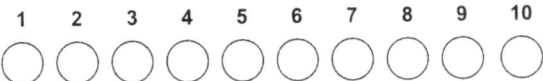

I take regular vacations and time away from preaching.

I have daily habits that support emotional, spiritual, and physical health.

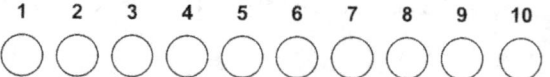

I engage in monthly or quarterly retreats for reflection and renewal.

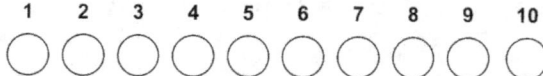

I maintain a sustainable pace across busy and quiet seasons of ministry.

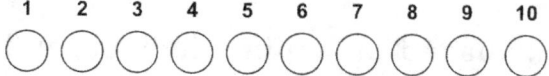

D. Delegation and Shared Ministry

I am comfortable delegating responsibilities to others.

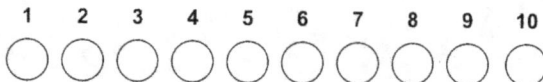

I equip and empower leaders effectively.

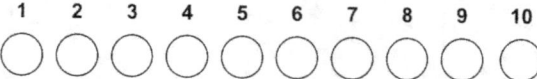

My church does not rely solely on me for ministry execution.

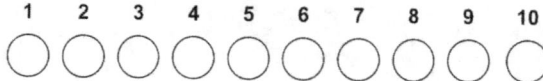

I regularly assess which tasks should no longer be mine.

I celebrate and affirm those who share the work of ministry.

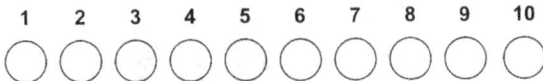

E. Emotional and Spiritual Alignment

I do not feel defined by the expectations of others.

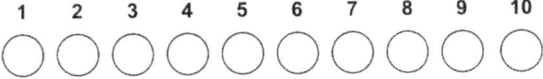

I feel rooted in my identity in Christ, not in ministry performance.

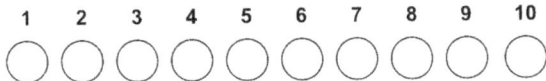

I consistently experience joy and fulfillment in my calling.

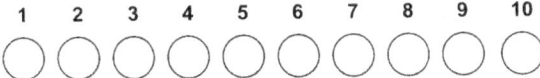

My spiritual life is nourished outside of sermon preparation.

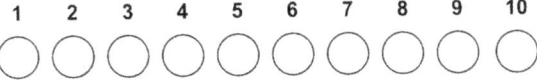

I feel emotionally present and available to my family and loved ones.

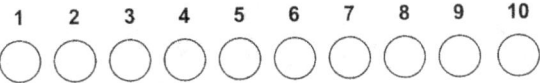

Add up total score and refer to the chart on the next page

BURNOUT RISK LEVELS

250-200	Strong resilience, healthy boundaries. Continue refining practices and mentoring others.
199-150	Generally healthy with areas needing attention. Identify specific adjustments.
149-100	Noticeable risk of fatigue or burnout. Consider accountability, coaching, or schedule restructuring.
Less than 100	High vulnerability to burnout. Seek intentional support and implement immediate changes.

Philip G Andrade

For through the grace given to me I say to each one among you not to think more highly of himself than he ought to think; but to think so as to have sound thinking, as God has allotted to each a measure of faith. For just as we have many members in one body and all the members do not have the same function, so we, who are many, are one body in Christ, and individually members one of another. Romans 12:3-5

FORMED FOR MINISTRY

09

FORMED FOR MINISTRY

Let us search out and examine our ways, And let us return to Yahweh.
Lamentations 3:40

Without knowledge of self, there is no knowledge of God. Our wisdom,
insofar as it ought to be deemed true and solid wisdom, consists almost
entirely of two parts: the knowledge of God and of ourselves.
John Calvin (Institutes)

HOW GOD FORMED YOU FOR MINISTRY

UNDERSTANDING LEADERSHIP EMERGENCE THEORY

Dr. J. Robert Clinton, longtime professor at Fuller Theological Seminary, developed Leadership Emergence Theory through extensive research of over 900 case studies of Christian leaders—biblical, historical, and contemporary figures including Hudson Taylor, Andrew Murray, A.W. Tozer, Dawson Trottman, and countless missionaries and national leaders from around the world.

His foundational insight emerged from decades of comparative analysis: "Leadership emergence is a lifetime process in which God intervenes throughout in crucial ways to shape that leader towards his purposes for the leader.

" This perspective revolutionized how we understand Christian leader-
ship development by revealing that God's shaping is neither random nor

merely circumstantial—it is intentional and purposeful.[1]

THE THREE FOUNDATIONAL CONCEPTS

Clinton's theory rests on three major concepts that explain how leaders develop:

1. Processing - *"God's intervention or shaping is intentional. His processing develops the leader's capacity*[2]*."*

God uses specific incidents, people, circumstances, and challenges—what Clinton calls "process items"—to shape leadership character, skills, and values. Clinton has identified approximately 50 distinct process items that commonly occur across leaders' lives, including integrity checks, isolation periods, conflicts, mentoring relationships, and ministry tasks.

2. Time Analysis - Leadership development occurs in identifiable phases over a lifetime. Clinton synthesized a "Ministry Time-Line" from hundreds of leaders' stories, revealing predictable developmental seasons from Sovereign Foundations through Inner-Life Growth, Ministry Maturing, Life Maturing, and ultimately Convergence.

3. Response Patterns - How leaders respond to God's processing significantly impacts their development trajectory. Clinton's research led to this crucial finding: "The time of development of a leader depends to some extent upon response to processing. Rapid recognition and positive response to God's processing speeds up development. Slower recognition or negative response delays development."

THE THREE-FOLD DEVELOPMENT GOAL

Clinton discovered that all processing ultimately moves toward three major leadership development goals:

1. Spiritual Formation - The development of leadership character and intimacy with God

2. Ministerial Formation - The development of influence means and ministry skills

3. Strategic Formation - The development of leadership values that culminate in a focused ministry philosophy and ultimate contribution

[1] Clinton Leadership. The Emerging Leader. Accessed December 28, 2025. https://clintonleadership.com/resources/complimentary/TheEmergingLeader.pdf. 1.
[2] Clinton, J. Robert. Leadership Emergence Theory: A Self-Study Manual for Analyzing the Development of a Christian Leader. 1989. Barnabas Publishers. 7.

As Clinton explains, *"Three major factors (processing, time, and leader response patterns) interweave together as God shapes a leader spiritually, ministerially, and strategically over a lifetime to bring about His purposes and resulting ultimate contribution[3]."*

WHY THIS MATTERS

Understanding Leadership Emergence Theory provides several critical benefits:

Personal Orientation - You can identify where you are in your development journey and what God may be doing in your current season.

Realistic Expectations - You'll understand that certain challenges are normal and even necessary for growth.

Proactive Participation - When you recognize process items, you can respond more intentionally to God's shaping.

Mentoring Wisdom - You can help others navigate their development with greater insight.

Clinton's research reminds us of the biblical mandate in Hebrews 13:7-8 to learn from those who have gone before us. By studying how God has developed leaders throughout history, we gain wisdom for our own journey and confidence that Jesus remains the same source of leadership power today.

The next section serves as an introduction to Leadershop Emergence Theory. It is strongly suggested that the reader obtain Clinton's *The Making of a Leader* for further insight, study and application.

LEADERSHIP EMERGENCE THEORY WORKSHEETS

This section will help you identify where you are in your leadership journey and create an intentional plan for growth. Take your time with each section, pray for insight, and be honest in your reflections. The goal is not perfection but awareness—recognizing how God has been working and how you can better cooperate with His developmental purposes for your life. Keep in mind the core principle:

[3] Ibid.

Leadership development is a lifelong process where God uses various experiences, people, and circumstances to shape leaders for their divine purposes.

PART 1: LEADERSHIP PHASE ASSESSMENT

Clinton identifies six phases in a leader's development. Read each description and check the phase that best describes your current season. For most readers of this volume you will find yourself in the latter phases. I've included all for reference and the chance that some young pastors might find their way here.

Phase 1: Sovereign Foundations (Birth - Late Teens/Early 20s)

- God is establishing my foundational character and values
- I'm being shaped by family, culture, and early spiritual experiences
- Early life experiences are forming my basic perspective on life and leadership

Phase 2: Inner-Life Growth (Variable Duration)

- I'm learning to walk with God personally
- Character development is a primary focus
- I'm experiencing tests that reveal and refine my integrity
- Ministry skills are developing but character is the main emphasis

Phase 3: Ministry Maturing (Variable Duration)

- I'm actively serving and discovering my spiritual gifts
- I'm learning what I'm good at and what brings life
- I'm experiencing both successes and failures in ministry
- I'm discovering my leadership style and strengths

Phase 4: Life Maturing (Variable Duration)

- I'm being refined through deeper tests and challenges

- I'm learning to trust God in isolation or difficult circumstances
- My relationship with God is deepening significantly
- I sense God pruning and redirecting my life and ministry

Phase 5: Convergence (Variable Duration)
- My gifts, experience, and opportunities are aligning
- I have unusual fruitfulness in a focused area of ministry
- I sense I'm doing what I was "made to do"
- My role and calling feel clear and integrated

Phase 6: Afterglow/Celebration (Later Years)
- I'm focused on indirect influence and mentoring
- My primary contribution is wisdom and perspective
- I'm celebrating God's faithfulness over my lifetime
- I'm investing in the next generation of leaders

My Current Phase: _____

PART 2: PROCESS ITEMS ASSESSMENT

Clinton identifies various "process items" God uses to develop leaders. Rate how significantly each has impacted your leadership development. write in 1=minimal though 5=transformational.

FORMED FOR MINISTRY

Foundational Process Items

- Integrity Check - Situations testing my character & consistency: ____
- Obedience Check - Tests of my willingness to obey God: ____
- Word Check - Learning to understand and apply Scripture: ____
- Ministry Task - Specific assignments or responsibilities : ____

Growth Process Items

- Isolation - Periods of being set apart or alone: ____
- Conflict - Relational or organizational struggles: ____
- Life Crisis - Major life disruptions or challenges: ____
- Prayer Challenge - Seasons of intense prayer or spiritual warfare: ____

Maturing Process Items

- Authority Insights - Learning how spiritual authority works: ____
- Discernment - Growing in wisdom and spiritual perception: ____
- Influence Challenge - Opportunities to influence beyond my role: ____
- Networking - Strategic relationships with other leaders: ____

Which process item has taught you the most? Why?

PART 3: DEVELOPMENT TASK ANALYSIS

For each development task, assess your current level of maturity. Score 1-10 from not at all mature to very mature.

- Ministry Philosophy. How clear are you on your core convictions about ministry and leadership?____

- Spiritual Authority. How well do you understand and operate in God-given authority?: ____

- Discernment. How developed is your ability to perceive spiritual dynamics and make wise decisions?: ____

- Giftedness. How clear are you on your spiritual gifts and how to use them effectively?: ____

- Destiny. How much clarity do you have about your ultimate contribution and calling?: ____

Area needing most attention: _____

PART 4: LEADERSHIP FORMATION REFLECTION QUESTIONS

Take time to thoughtfully answer these questions:

1. Leadership Timeline

What are 5-7 key events or experiences that have significantly shaped you as a leader?

Looking at your past, what patterns do you see in how God has developed you?

3. Current Processing

What is God currently using to develop you? What is He teaching you?

4. Ministry Burden

What issue, need, or group of people do you care most deeply about?

5. Ultimate Contribution

If you could be remembered for one thing in your leadership, what would it be?

6. Barriers and Obstacles

What internal or external barriers are hindering your leadership development?

PART 5: PERSONAL LEADERSHIP DEVELOPMENT PLAN

My Leadership Vision Statement

In one paragraph, describe what you sense God calling you to become and do as a leader.

PRIORITY DEVELOPMENT AREAS (NEXT 12 MONTHS)

Character Development

Goal: _____

Action Steps:

1.

2.

3.

Accountability: Who will help me? _____

Skill Development

Goal: _____

Action Steps:

1.

2.

3.

Resources Needed:

Relational Development

Goal: _____

Key Relationships to Develop:

1.

2.

3.

How: _____

Spiritual Formation

Goal: _____

Spiritual Disciplines to Practice:

1.

2.

3.

Support System: _____

Ministry Focus Areas

Primary Ministry Arena: _____

Secondary Opportunities: _____

Ways to Increase Effectiveness:

1.

2.

3.

Learning Plan

Books to Read:

1.

2.

3.

People to Learn From (mentors, coaches, models):

1.

2.

3.

Experiences to Pursue:

1.

2.

3.

For I am confident of this very thing, that He who began a good work in you will perfect it until the day of Christ Jesus. Philippians 1:6

"Come away by yourselves to a desolate place and rest a while." (For there were many people coming and going, and they did not even have time to eat.) Mark 6:31

Let us search out and examine our ways,
And let us return to Yahweh.

Lamentations 3:40

FINAL THOUGHTS
THE LONG OBEDIENCE

Let us not lose heart in doing good, for in due time we will reap if we do not grow weary. Galatians 6:9

The photograph on the last page captures something essential about the pastoral life—ancient stones that have weathered centuries of storms, still standing, still bearing witness. Ministry, like those stones, is not measured in moments but in decades. Not in bursts of passionate energy but in faithful presence over the long haul.

When I began writing this book, I had just returned from a three-month sabbatical that quite literally saved my ministry. For forty years, I had been running—running to the next crisis, the next sermon, the next person in need. I had mistaken exhaustion for faithfulness and busyness for devotion. I thought burning out was the same as burning brightly. I was wrong.

The journey I've invited you on through these pages is the journey I'm still walking. I don't have this all figured out. There are still weeks when I say yes when I should say no, when I work through my day off, when I let the urgent crowd out the important. Old patterns die hard. But I'm learning—slowly, by grace—that sustainable ministry is not about perfection. It's about direction.

WHAT WE'VE LEARNED TOGETHER

Let's trace back through the ground we've covered, not to repeat ourselves but to remember. Because what we need most is not new information but renewed conviction.

PHYSICAL FOUNDATION

We began with our bodies because that's where ministry happens. You cannot love God with all your strength if you've destroyed the vessel He gave you to serve in. Sleep is not laziness—it's trust. Healthy eating is not vanity—it's stewardship. Exercise is not optional—it's wisdom. Friendship is not a luxury—it's survival. And Sabbath is not legalism—it's obedience to the rhythm God wrote into creation itself. Your body is a sanctuary of the Holy Spirit. When we treat it as such, we honor the One who dwells within.

SPIRITUAL VITALITY

From the physical, we moved to the spiritual—because a leader cannot lead others where they themselves refuse to go. Continued learning keeps us sharp and humble. Personal worship keeps us anchored in intimacy rather than performance. Accountability keeps us safe from the subtle drift toward compromise. And focusing on our spiritual gifts keeps us from the exhausting trap of trying to be all things to all people.

Ministry flows from intimacy with Jesus, not merely from skill or effort.

MENTAL HEALTH

Then we turned inward, to that hidden world of thought and emotion where leadership is won or lost. We confronted the dark side—those unhealed wounds and unmet needs that shape how we lead when we're not paying attention. We learned that renewal is not optional if we want to last. And we discovered that not every burden is ours to carry, that some responsibilities belong to others and some belong to God alone.

Guard your heart, for everything you do flows from it.

EMOTIONAL RESILIENCE

Ministry requires more than strong minds; it requires resilient hearts. We explored how to process criticism without becoming defensive or despairing. We learned that discouragement is not the same as failure and that fatigue is not the same as unfaithfulness. And we discovered that cultivating joy and gratitude is not superficial positivity—it's a spiritual discipline that guards our souls from bitterness.

Emotionally resilient leaders feel deeply, but they do not fall easily.

CERTAINTY OF CALLING

Perhaps no chapter matters more than the one on calling. Without a clear sense that God Himself has placed you in ministry, every criticism feels fatal and every difficulty seems final. But with that certainty—that deep conviction that you are where you're supposed to be, doing what you're supposed to do—you can endure almost anything.

The call of God is the anchor that holds steady when everything else is shaking.

THE BOUNDARIES WE NEED

From calling, we moved to limits. We learned that healthy boundaries are not walls that keep people out but fences that keep good things in. We discovered that saying no to some things is the only way to say yes to the right things. We confronted the messiah complex—that subtle belief that the church cannot survive without us—and learned that servant leadership is about empowering others, not exhausting ourselves.

Every yes carries a hidden no. The question is whether we will choose our nos intentionally or let them be chosen for us.

THE PROCESS OF FORMATION

Finally, we explored how God has been shaping you for ministry all along. Through Clinton's Leadership Emergence Theory, we saw that nothing has been wasted—not the wounds, not the waiting, not the wilderness seasons. God uses it all to form us into the leaders He created us to be.

Leadership development is a lifelong process where God uses various experiences, people, and circumstances to shape leaders for their divine purposes.

THE CENTRAL TRUTH

If there's one truth that runs through every chapter, every principle, it's this:

Only healthy pastors can sustain healthy ministry.

You cannot give what you do not have. You cannot lead others to rest if you never rest yourself. You cannot preach grace while living under the crushing weight of performance. You cannot shepherd God's people faithfully if you've neglected the sheep God gave you first—yourself and your family.

Self-care is not selfish. It's stewardship.

Boundaries are not unfaithfulness. They're wisdom.

Rest is not optional. It's obedience.

THE PATH FORWARD

So where do we go from here? How do you take everything in these pages and translate it into Monday morning reality?

START SMALL

Don't try to fix everything at once. You didn't get here overnight, and you won't get healthy overnight. Pick one thing—just one—and commit to it for the next thirty days.

- Maybe it's protecting your day off.
- Maybe it's scheduling regular exercise.
- Maybe it's finding an accountability partner.
- Maybe it's learning to say no without guilt.
- Maybe it's carving out daily time for personal worship that's not sermon prep.

Start small. Start somewhere. But start.

GET HELP

You cannot do this alone. That's the whole point of this book—we were never meant to carry these burdens by ourselves. Find a mentor, a counselor, a coach, or a trusted friend who can walk this journey with you. Share your struggles. Confess your fears. Ask for help. The strongest leaders are not those who need no one but those who are humble enough to admit they need everyone. If you're burned out or close to it, don't be ashamed to seek professional help. Therapy is not failure—it's courage. Medical intervention is not weakness—it's the best choice when needed. God uses doctors and counselors just as surely as He uses Scripture and prayer.

INVOLVE YOUR CHURCH

If you're a senior pastor or lead elder, bring your leadership team into this conversation. Share your scores from the assessments in this book. Admit where you're struggling. Ask for their support in creating healthier rhythms and clearer boundaries. Churches that love their pastors protect their pastors. But they can only protect what they know about. Give them permission to care for you the way you care for them.

REMEMBER YOUR FAMILY

Your family paid a price for you to be in ministry. Don't let that price be their relationship with you or with the church. Make time for your spouse—real time, not distracted time. Be present with your children. Model for them what it looks like to follow Jesus without sacrificing the people you love most on the altar of ministry.

The best gift you can give your congregation is a healthy marriage and children who don't resent the church.

TRUST GOD'S SOVEREIGNTY

Finally—and this may be the hardest thing—trust that God is bigger than your limitations. The church belongs to Him, not to you. He will accomplish His purposes whether you're at your desk or on sabbatical, whether you're leading the meeting or someone else is, whether you're preaching or resting.

When you rest, you're not being irresponsible. You're trusting that God can sustain His church while you sleep, while you play, while you invest in your family. That's not laziness—that's faith.

A PERSONAL WORD

I'm writing these final words from my desk overlooking the church I've served for many years. There have been seasons when I wondered if I would make it, times when the weight seemed too heavy and the criticism too sharp. There have been moments when I questioned my calling and days when I wanted to quit.

But God has been faithful. Not because I've been perfect—I haven't. Not because I've always had clear boundaries—I haven't. Not because I've never made mistakes—I have, more than I can count.

God has been faithful because that's who He is. And the journey toward health—toward sustainable, life-giving, long-term ministry—has been worth every difficult conversation, every hard boundary, every moment of learning to let go.

I'm still here. Still preaching. Still shepherding. Still learning. Still grow-ing. And I want the same for you.

YOUR NEXT STEP

So here's what I want you to do right now, before you close this book and move on to the next thing on your list:

Stop!

Take a deep breath.

Thank God for calling you to this beautiful, impossible, life-giving work.

Ask Him to show you one thing—just one thing—that needs to change in how you're living and serving.

Then do it.

Not tomorrow. Not next week. Today.

Your congregation needs you healthy. Your family needs you present. And God deserves leaders who trust Him enough to rest.

The stones on the Parthenon have stood for centuries not because they never faced storms but because they were built to last. They had a solid

205

foundation. They were made of material that could endure.

That's what God wants to build in you—not flashy, not impressive, but enduring. Faithful. Present. Sustainable.

For the long haul.

For the glory of God.

For the good of His church.

So...Serve faithfully. Rest deeply. And trust that the One who called you will sustain you every step of the way.

For I am confident of this very thing, that He who began a good work in you will perfect it until the day of Christ Jesus.
Philippians 1:6

*The footsteps of a man are
established by Yahweh.
And he delights in his way.*

Psalm 37:23

ABOUT THE AUTHOR

Phillip Andrade has spent more than forty years in ministry—long enough to have been a shepherd to teenagers, served as a missionary in Japan, and weathered two long-term senior pastorates in New England without losing his sanity or his sense of humor. Along the way, he earned a B.A. in Archaeology, an M.Div. in Theology, and a D.Min. in Leadership Development, proving that he is both somewhat educated and capable of sitting through very long monotone lectures.

To support his pastoral habit over the years, he has moonlighted as a police officer, graphic designer, and firearms instructor—which means he can preach a sermon, design the bulletin, and arrest you for not reading it thoroughly. He also dabbles in bladesmithing because nothing says "well-rounded pastor" like forging sharp objects.

He and his wife have been married for over forty years, have four children, and enjoy a plethora of grandchildren—a biblical word meaning "more than you can conveniently count." Now embracing the role of author, he brings together wisdom, shenanigans, and the wounds of ministry to encourage others to follow Jesus fully.

You can follow him, if you dare, at www.phillipandrade.com

RESTORED TO LEAD

LIST OF PHOTOGRAPHS

www.ingramcontent.com/pod-product-compliance
Lightning Source LLC
Chambersburg PA
CBHW080901120626
46555CB00008B/2901